Fish and Seafood

Marshall Cavendish London & New York

Edited by Isabel Moore

Published by
Marshall Cavendish Publications Limited
58 Old Compton Street
London W1V 5PA

© Marshall Cavendish Limited 1973, 1974, 1975, 1976

This material was first published by
Marshall Cavendish Limited
in the partwork *Supercook*

This volume first published 1976

Printed by Henri Proost, Turnhout, Belgium

ISBN 0 85685 164 7

Contents

Key to symbols

☆ This is a guide to each recipe's preparation and cooking

    ☆ **Easy**

    ☆ ☆ **Requires special care**

☆ ☆ ☆ **Complicated**

① This is a guide to the cost of each dish and will, of course, vary according to region and season.

    ① **Inexpensive**

    ① ① **Reasonable**

① ① ① **Expensive**

⧖ This is a guide to the preparation and cooking time required for each dish and will vary according to the skill of the individual cook.

    ⧖ **Less than 1 hour**

    ⧖ ⧖ **1 hour to $2\frac{1}{2}$ hours**

⧖ ⧖ ⧖ **Over $2\frac{1}{2}$ hours**

Basic metric conversions

Solid measures

15 grams	=	$\frac{1}{2}$ ounce
25 grams	=	1 ounce
50 grams	=	2 ounces
125 grams	=	4 ounces
225 grams	=	8 ounces
450 grams	=	1 pound
1 kilogram	=	2 pounds 2 ounces

Liquid measures

25 millilitres	=	1 fluid ounce
50 millilitres	=	2 fluid ounces
125 millilitres	=	4 fluid ounces
150 millilitres	=	5 fluid ounces
300 millilitres	=	10 fluid ounces
600 millilitres	=	1 pint
1 litre	=	$1\frac{3}{4}$ pints

Linear measures

0·6 centimetre	=	$\frac{1}{4}$ inch
1·3 centimetres	=	$\frac{1}{2}$ inch
2·5 centimetres	=	1 inch
10 centimetres	=	4 inches
15 centimetres	=	6 inches
23 centimetres	=	9 inches
30 centimetres	=	1 foot
1 metre	=	40 inches

American equivalents of food and measurements are shown in brackets.

Fish and seafood for the family

Fish and Seafood have long formed part of our basic diet. But they are a relatively small part, which is rather surprising when you consider their comparative cheapness and high protein value.

Traditional attitudes to cooking fish are probably partly to blame — all too often, it's dip-it-in-flour-or-batter and fry-it-to-kingdom-come! Some fish can be just as easily poached or baked; and they can form the basis of exotically different (but marvellously tasty!) dishes as well as of flavourful familiar ones. We think you'll agree when you see (and sample) our simple, straightforward recipes like Herrings in Butter Sauce (page 8) and Potted Shrimps or Prawns (page 28). Compare them with 'new' tastes such as Chinese Deep-Fried Prawns (page 26) and Fillets of Cod with Caper Sauce (pictured below, recipe page 2).

Tasty meals needn't cost the earth, as most of our recipes prove. But, there are occasions in every family when there's a bit extra to spend and when something special is called for. The recipes in **For Special Occasions** are absolutely superb to eat and elegant enough to enhance the finest table.

All of our recipes — the inexpensive, everyday as well as the more special ones — are attractive to look at and good to eat. And, with the busy mum in mind, they have been specially selected so that their preparation won't wear her to a frazzle; food is meant to be enjoyed by ALL who eat it, including the cook!

1

Cod

Cod Bake

☆ ☆   ① 　 　 ✕ ✕

Tasty and easy to prepare, Cod Bake is an unusual way to serve cod. Accompany with parsley potatoes.

6 SERVINGS

1 tablespoon butter
2 lb. cod fillets, skinned
1 small onion, finely chopped
1 celery stalk, finely chopped
½ green pepper, white pith removed, seeded and finely chopped
3 oz. [½ cup] walnuts, chopped
3 tablespoons chopped fresh parsley
6 tablespoons dry white breadcrumbs
¼ teaspoon black pepper
⅛ teaspoon Tabasco sauce
1 teaspoon Worcestershire sauce
1 teaspoon dried tarragon
2 eggs, separated
4 fl. oz. single cream [½ cup light cream]
4 oz. [½ cup] butter, melted

COURT BOUILLON

16 fl. oz. [2 cups] water
3 parsley sprigs
1 small onion, finely chopped
6 peppercorns
½ teaspoon salt
 juice of ½ lemon

SAUCE

2½ oz. [5 tablespoons] butter
3 tablespoons flour
½ teaspoon salt
¼ teaspoon white pepper
2 hard-boiled eggs, chopped
2 tablespoons single [light] cream

This delicious Cod Bake makes a super family dinner.

Preheat the oven to fairly hot 375°F (Gas Mark 5, 190°C).

Grease a medium-sized ovenproof dish with the tablespoon of butter.

To make the court bouillon, pour the water into a large saucepan. Add the parsley, onion, peppercorns, salt and lemon juice and place the pan over high heat. Bring the court bouillon to the boil, reduce the heat to moderately low and add the cod fillets to the pan. Simmer the cod for 12 to 15 minutes, or until it flakes easily.

Transfer the cod to a chopping board. Reserve the court bouillon. Allow the fish to cool slightly, then remove the skin and using a fork, flake the fish.

Strain the court bouillon into a measuring jug and reserve 12 fluid ounces [1½ cups].

In a large bowl, mix together the cod, onion, celery, green pepper, walnuts, parsley, breadcrumbs, pepper, Tabasco, Worcestershire and tarragon.

In a small bowl, beat the egg yolks with a fork until they are pale yellow. Stir the yolks into the cod mixture and then blend in the cream and melted butter.

In a medium-sized bowl, beat the egg whites with a wire whisk or rotary beater until they form stiff peaks. With a metal spoon, carefully fold them into the cod mixture. Turn the mixture into the prepared dish. Place the dish in the oven and bake for 40 minutes or until firm.

While the cod mixture is baking, prepare the sauce. In a small heavy saucepan, melt 1½ ounces [3 tablespoons] of the butter over moderate heat. Remove the pan from the heat, and with a wooden spoon, stir in the flour, salt and pepper. Replace the pan on the heat and, stirring constantly, gradually add the reserved court bouillon. Cook and stir the sauce for 5 minutes or until it has thickened and

is smooth. Remove the pan from the heat.

Stir the remaining butter into the sauce. When the butter has been incorporated, stir in the eggs and cream.

When the cod bake is cooked, remove it from the oven and serve immediately, with the sauce.

Fillets of Cod with Caper Sauce

☆ 　 　 ① ①　 　 ✕

This attractive dish (pictured on page 1) *makes a superb meal served with croquette potatoes.*

3 SERVINGS

6 small cod fillets, skinned
10 fl. oz. [1¼ cups] fish stock
5 fl. oz. [⅝ cup] dry white wine
¼ teaspoon salt
¼ teaspoon black pepper
¼ teaspoon grated nutmeg
1 teaspoon cornflour [cornstarch] dissolved in 1 tablespoon water

$\frac{1}{8}$ teaspoon cayenne pepper
5 fl. oz. double cream [$\frac{5}{8}$ cup heavy cream]
2 tablespoons capers
6 to 9 large cooked prawns

Roll up each cod fillet and fasten the rolls with thick thread. Lay the rolled fillets in the bottom of a medium-sized heavy saucepan. Pour over the fish stock, wine, salt, pepper and nutmeg. Place the pan over moderate heat and bring the liquid to the boil. Reduce the heat to low, cover the pan and simmer for 20 minutes. Remove the pan from the heat.

Remove the fish fillets from the pan. Remove and discard the thread. Arrange the rolls in a serving dish and keep hot while you finish the sauce.

Return the pan to moderate heat and bring the cooking juices to the boil. Boil for 10 minutes. Stir in the cornflour [cornstarch] and cayenne. Cook the sauce, stirring constantly, for 3 minutes, or until it is thick. Reduce the heat to low and stir in the cream and capers. Continue cooking, stirring constantly, for 3 minutes. Do not allow the sauce to boil.

Remove the pan from the heat and pour the sauce over the fish rolls. Garnish with the prawns and serve.

Cod Steaks with Tomatoes and Anchovies

This is an attractive and exceptionally tasty way of serving cod.

4 SERVINGS

2 fl. oz. [$\frac{1}{4}$ cup] olive oil
1 small onion, thinly sliced
1 garlic clove, chopped
1 green pepper, white pith removed, seeded and thinly sliced
2 oz. canned anchovies, drained and chopped
2 oz. [$\frac{2}{3}$ cup] black olives, stoned
$\frac{1}{8}$ teaspoon fennel seed
8 x 4 oz. cod steaks
3 small tomatoes, thinly sliced
$\frac{1}{2}$ teaspoon salt
$\frac{1}{4}$ teaspoon black pepper
2$\frac{1}{2}$ oz. canned tomato purée

4 fl. oz. [$\frac{1}{2}$ cup] dry red wine

Preheat the oven to fairly hot 400°F (Gas Mark 6, 200°C).

In a medium-sized frying-pan, heat half the olive oil over moderate heat. When the oil is hot, add the onion, garlic and green pepper. Cook them for 5 to 7 minutes, stirring occasionally, or until the onion is soft and translucent but not brown. Remove the pan from the heat and stir in the anchovies, olives and fennel.

Place four of the cod steaks in a greased dish and spread the anchovy mixture over them. Top each steak with another cod steak. Arrange the tomatoes on top. Brush the tomatoes with the remaining oil, salt and pepper.

In a small bowl, combine the tomato purée with the wine. Pour the mixture over the fish. Place the dish in the oven and bake for 30 minutes, basting twice. Serve at once.

Colourful Cod Steaks with Tomatoes and Anchovies.

Haddock

and serve at once, straight from the casserole.

Haddock Croquettes in Hot Sauce

Tender Haddock Croquettes, simmered in a spicy sauce, makes an excellent hors d'oeuvre or, served on a bed of rice with a tossed green salad, they are a sustaining meal.

4 SERVINGS

1 lb. haddock, cooked, cooled, skinned, boned and flaked
1 teaspoon salt
½ teaspoon black pepper
1½ oz. [¾ cup] fresh white breadcrumbs
2 tablespoons finely chopped fresh parsley
1 egg, lightly beaten
3 tablespoons flour

SAUCE

1 medium-sized onion, finely chopped
½ teaspoon ground ginger
½ teaspoon ground coriander
¼ teaspoon ground turmeric
⅛ teaspoon hot chilli powder
2 oz. [¼ cup] butter
2 tablespoons vegetable oil
5 fl. oz. [⅝ cup] dry white wine
5 fl. oz. [⅝ cup] fish stock
4 lemon wedges

In a medium-sized mixing bowl, combine the fish, ½ teaspoon of the salt, the pepper, breadcrumbs and 1 tablespoon of the chopped parsley. Add the egg and mix it in thoroughly.

With your hands, shape the mixture into about 10 small croquettes. Put the flour on a board or large plate. Roll the croquettes gently in the flour to coat them on all sides.

Place the croquettes in the refrigerator to chill for at least 45 minutes.

In a small mixing bowl, mix together the onion, ginger, coriander, turmeric, chilli powder, remaining parsley and remaining salt. Set aside.

In a large frying-pan, melt the butter with the oil over moderate heat. When the foam subsides, add the onion and spice mixture. Cook, stirring frequently, for 5 to 7 minutes or until the onion is soft but not brown. Pour in the wine and fish stock. Bring the sauce to the boil, stirring constantly. Reduce the heat to low and simmer the sauce for 2 to 3 minutes.

Gently arrange the croquettes in the pan and baste them with the sauce. Cook the croquettes for 6 to 8 minutes on each

Haddock with Cider

A pleasant and unusual dish, Haddock with Cider is delicious served for a family lunch or supper with parsley potatoes, buttered carrots and, perhaps, a mixed green salad. Chilled cider would make a good accompanying drink.

4 SERVINGS

8 fl. oz. [1 cup] cider
2 medium-sized onions, thinly sliced
1 green pepper, white pith removed, seeded and coarsely chopped
1½ lb. fresh or frozen and thawed haddock fillets, skinned
3 medium-sized tomatoes, blanched, peeled and coarsely chopped
2 teaspoons chopped fresh marjoram or 1 teaspoon dried marjoram
⅛ teaspoon cayenne pepper
1½ teaspoons salt
½ teaspoon freshly ground white pepper
3 tablespoons fresh white breadcrumbs
1 oz. [¼ cup] Parmesan cheese, grated

Preheat the oven to warm 325°F (Gas

Served with rice, Haddock Croquettes in Hot Sauce make a spicy meal.

Mark 3, 170°C).

In a medium-sized saucepan, bring the cider to the boil over moderate heat. Add the onions and green pepper, reduce the heat to low and simmer the mixture for 5 minutes, or until the cider has reduced by about one-quarter. Remove the pan from the heat.

On a chopping board, cut the fish into 3- or 4-inch pieces and put them into a flameproof casserole. Add the cider mixture and tomatoes and mix well to blend. Sprinkle the marjoram, cayenne, salt and pepper over the mixture. Cover the casserole and place it over moderately high heat. Bring the liquid to the boil. Transfer the casserole to the oven and bake for 20 to 25 minutes, or until the fish flakes very easily when tested with a fork. Remove the casserole from the oven.

Preheat the grill [broiler] to high.

In a small bowl, combine the breadcrumbs and grated cheese together and spread the mixture over the fish. Place the casserole under the grill [broiler] and grill [broil] the mixture for 4 minutes, or until the topping browns and the cheese melts.

Remove the casserole from the heat

4

side or until they are evenly browned. Baste the croquettes with the sauce frequently during the cooking period.

With a slotted spoon, lift the croquettes out of the pan and arrange them on a warmed serving dish. Pour the sauce over the croquettes and garnish with the lemon wedges.

Serve at once.

Swedish Summer Casserole

A tasty and economical dish suitable for lunch or supper, Swedish Summer Casserole may be served with parsley potatoes and a tossed green salad.

6-8 SERVINGS

3 lb. fresh or frozen and thawed haddock fillets, skinned
1 teaspoon salt
1 tablespoon finely chopped fresh parsley
2 tablespoons finely chopped fresh chives
1 oz. [2 tablespoons] butter blended with 2 tablespoons flour juice of 1 lemon
4 tomatoes, thickly sliced

Sprinkle the fillets with the salt and place them in a flameproof casserole. Sprinkle over the parsley and chives and dot the fish with the butter mixture. Add the lemon juice and pour in just enough water to come about halfway up the sides of the fish.

Place the casserole over moderate heat and bring the liquid to the boil. Reduce the heat to low, cover the casserole and simmer for 10 minutes. Place the sliced tomatoes over the fish and simmer for a further 5 minutes or until the fish flesh flakes easily when tested with a fork.

Remove the casserole from the heat and serve immediately, straight from the casserole.

Swedish Summer Casserole is as good to eat as it is refreshing to look at! Serve with lots of green salad.

Haddock Soufflé is easy to make!

Finnan Haddie

The name Finnan Haddie is derived from Findon haddock. Many centuries ago, there was a glut of haddock in the small Scottish fishing port of Findon, and the housewives discovered the process of smoking the haddock in order to preserve it.

4 SERVINGS

2 lb. smoked haddock
1 large onion, sliced
1 pint [2½ cups] milk
½ teaspoon black pepper
1 oz. [2 tablespoons] butter, cut into small pieces

Place the haddock and onion in a medium-sized saucepan. Add enough milk just to cover the fish, the pepper and butter.

Place the pan over moderate heat and bring the milk slowly to the boil.

Cover the pan, reduce the heat to low and simmer gently for 10 minutes, or until the fish flakes easily.

Remove the pan from the heat. To serve, pour a little of the cooking liquid over the fish.

Haddock Soufflé

A souffléd fish dish, Haddock Soufflé is ideal for luncheon or supper when served with a green salad. If you would like to serve this dish as part of a special dinner, as a savoury or fish course, use a medium-sized soufflé dish and allow another 5 minutes cooking time.

3-4 SERVINGS

10 fl. oz. [1¼ cups] water
10 oz. smoked or fresh haddock
1 teaspoon butter
2 tablespoons flour
5 fl. oz. [⅝ cup] milk
2 oz. [½ cup] Cheddar cheese, grated
1 teaspoon grated lemon rind
¼ teaspoon dried or 1 teaspoon chopped fresh dill
¼ teaspoon salt
¼ teaspoon black pepper
2 egg yolks
3 egg whites

In a large frying-pan, heat the water and fish over moderate heat. When the water begins to simmer, reduce the heat to low, cover the pan and cook for 12 minutes or until the fish flakes easily when tested with a fork. Remove the pan from the heat and, with a slotted spoon, transfer the fish to a plate. Flake it and discard the skin and any bones. Reserve 5 fluid ounces [⅝ cup] of the cooking liquid.

Preheat the oven to fairly hot 375°F (Gas Mark 5, 190°C).

Using the butter, grease a medium-sized deep pie dish. Set aside.

In a medium-sized saucepan, mix together half the reserved cooking liquid and the flour with a wooden spoon to make a smooth paste. Stir in the remaining cooking liquid and the milk. Place the pan over moderate heat and, stirring constantly bring to the boil. Boil the sauce for 2 minutes.

Remove the pan from the heat and set aside to cool slightly. Stir in the fish, the cheese, lemon rind, dill, salt and pepper. Beat in the egg yolks. Set aside.

In a large mixing bowl, beat the egg whites with a wire whisk or rotary beater until they form stiff peaks.

With a metal spoon, carefully fold the egg whites into the fish mixture. Spoon the mixture into the pie dish.

Place the dish in the oven and bake for 30 minutes or until the soufflé is well risen and a deep golden brown.

Remove the soufflé from the oven and serve immediately.

Hake with Ham and Egg Stuffing

This unusual way of cooking hake originated in Spain, where the fish is known as merluza. Serve it with sautéed potatoes and courgettes [zucchini], and a light white wine such as a good Spanish Chablis.

6 SERVINGS

2 hard-boiled eggs
6 oz. lean cooked ham, finely chopped
4 tablespoons stoned and chopped black olives
2 tablespoons finely chopped fresh parsley
2 teaspoons salt
½ teaspoon freshly ground black pepper
1 x 4 to 5 lb. hake, cleaned, with the backbone removed and the head and tail left on
1 teaspoon olive oil
4 large tomatoes, sliced
1 bay leaf

Preheat the oven to moderate 350°F (Gas Mark 4, 180°C).

In a small bowl, mash the hard-boiled eggs with a fork. Add the ham, olives, parsley, ½ teaspoon salt and ¼ teaspoon of pepper and mix well. Set the stuffing aside.

Wash the fish under cold running water and dry it thoroughly on kitchen paper towels. Place the fish on a wooden board and sprinkle 1 teaspoon of salt over it.

Line a baking dish, large enough to hold the fish, with aluminium foil, overlapping the ends so that they may be used to enclose the fish. With the oil, lightly grease the foil.

Using a metal spoon, fill the fish with the prepared stuffing. Sew or skewer the fish together and place it in the prepared baking dish. Cover the fish with layers of tomatoes, and sprinkle over the remaining salt and pepper. Tuck the bay leaf between the layers and close the foil tightly.

Place the dish in the centre of the oven and bake for 1 hour. Remove the dish from the oven and transfer the whole fish to a warmed serving dish. Unwrap the aluminium foil. Arrange the tomatoes over and around the fish and serve immediately.

Hake with Ham and Egg Stuffing is an economical - and unusual - way of cooking this superb fish.

Herrings in Butter Sauce

A simple yet delicious lunch or supper dish, Herrings in Butter Sauce is very good served with boiled new potatoes.

4 SERVINGS

4 large herrings, filleted
6½ tablespoons seasoned flour, made with 6 tablespoons flour, 1 teaspoon salt and ½ teaspoon black pepper
3 oz. [⅜ cup] butter
2 teaspoons lemon juice
1 tablespoon chopped fresh parsley

Wash the herring fillets under cold running water and pat them dry with kitchen paper towels.

Place the seasoned flour on a plate and, one by one, dip the herring fillets into it, shaking off any excess flour. Set aside.

In a large frying-pan, melt the butter over moderate heat. When the foam subsides, add the herring fillets to the pan and cook them for 3 minutes on each side, or until they are lightly browned and the flesh flakes easily when tested with a fork.

Remove the pan from the heat and, with a slotted spoon, transfer the herrings from the pan to a warmed serving dish.

So simple to make, so delicious to eat - Herrings in Butter Sauce.

Spoon over the lemon juice, then the pan juices.

Sprinkle over the parsley and serve at once.

Herrings with Mustard Sauce

Sometimes the simple things of life are the best — even in cooking! This recipe for Herrings with Mustard Sauce is an excellent example as it makes an economical family meal that is really delicious.

6 SERVINGS

6 large herrings, filleted
1 tablespoon lemon juice
2 eggs, lightly beaten
2 teaspoons dry mustard
½ teaspoon salt
¼ teaspoon black pepper
2 oz. [½ cup] flour
3 oz. [⅜ cup] butter
6 lemon wedges
MUSTARD SAUCE
4 oz. [½ cup] butter
½ teaspoon salt
¼ teaspoon white pepper
1 teaspoon dry mustard

Wash the herring fillets under cold running water and pat them dry with kitchen paper towels. Sprinkle the herrings with the lemon juice and set aside.

In a shallow bowl, combine the eggs,

mustard, salt and pepper, beating with a fork until the ingredients are well blended. Sprinkle the flour on to a plate or a sheet of greaseproof or waxed paper.

Dip the fillets, one at a time, in the egg mixture, then roll them in the flour, coating them on all sides. Set aside.

In a large frying-pan, melt the butter over moderate heat. When the foam subsides, add the fillets and cook them for 3 minutes on each side, or until the flesh flakes easily when tested with a fork. Remove the pan from the heat and transfer the fillets to a warmed serving plate. Keep warm while you make the sauce.

In a small saucepan, melt the butter over low heat. Stir in the salt, pepper and mustard and beat the mixture with a fork or spoon until the ingredients are well blended. Remove the pan from the heat and pour the sauce over the herrings.

Garnish with the lemon wedges and serve at once.

Herrings Stuffed with Rice

Herrings Stuffed with Rice is a superb dish of herrings stuffed with sweetcorn, bacon, rice and cream, baked with wine.

4 SERVINGS

2 oz. [¼ cup] butter
4 large herrings, cleaned and gutted

1 lemon, quartered
1 teaspoon salt
½ teaspoon black pepper
2 lean bacon slices, diced
1 small onion, finely chopped
3 oz. [1¼ cups] cooked rice
3 tablespoons drained sweetcorn kernels
4 tablespoons double [heavy] cream
1 parsley sprig, finely chopped
3 fl. oz. [⅜ cup] dry white wine

Preheat the oven to moderate 350°F (Gas Mark 4, 180°C).

Using 1 tablespoon of the butter, grease a large baking dish and set aside.

Wash the herrings and pat them dry with kitchen paper towels.

Rub the fish all over with the lemon pieces and discard the lemon. Rub ½ teaspoon of salt and ¼ teaspoon of pepper all over the fish.

In a small frying-pan, melt 1 tablespoon of the butter over moderate heat. When the foam subsides, add the bacon and fry, stirring occasionally, for 6 to 8 minutes, or until it is crisp. With a slotted spoon, remove the bacon from the pan and drain it on kitchen paper towels. Transfer the bacon to a medium-sized mixing bowl and set aside.

Add the onion to the frying-pan and cook, stirring occasionally, for 5 to 7 minutes, or until it is soft and translucent but not brown.

Remove the pan from the heat. With a slotted spoon, remove the onion from the pan and add it to the bacon.

Stir the rice, sweetcorn, cream, the remaining salt and pepper and the parsley into the bacon and onion. Combine the mixture thoroughly.

Using a metal spoon, stuff the fish with the rice mixture. Close the cavities with skewers, or a trussing needle and thread.

Arrange the fish in the baking dish. Pour over the wine and dot the fish with the remaining butter, in pieces.

Cover the dish with a lid or aluminium foil and place it in the centre of the oven. Bake for 45 minutes, basting occasionally, or until the fish flakes easily.

Remove the dish from the oven. Remove and discard the trussing thread or skewers and serve immediately.

Herring Roes in Devilled Sauce

☆   ①   ⧖

These devilled roes make an excellent snack.
2 SERVINGS

2 tablespoons flour
8 oz. soft herring roes
1 oz. [2 tablespoons] butter
1 small onion, finely chopped
1 green pepper, white pith removed, seeded and chopped
1 teaspoon curry powder

Herrings Stuffed with Rice makes an economical and nutritious family meal.

¼ teaspoon Worcestershire sauce
½ teaspoon black pepper
⅛ teaspoon cayenne pepper
¼ teaspoon dry mustard
1 tablespoon sweet mango chutney
2 tablespoons chicken stock
2 slices warm buttered toast

Put the flour on a small plate. Dip the roes in the flour and coat them all over.

In a small frying-pan, melt the butter over moderate heat. When the foam subsides, add the roes and fry them for 3 to 4 minutes, turning them frequently, or until they are lightly browned. With a slotted spoon, remove the roes from the pan and set them aside on a plate.

Add the onion to the pan and fry, stirring occasionally, for 5 to 7 minutes or until it is soft and translucent but not brown. Add the green pepper and curry powder and fry, stirring frequently, for 3 minutes. Stir in the Worcestershire, pepper, cayenne, mustard, chutney and stock. Cook the sauce for 1 minute. Return the roes to the pan and turn and toss them in the sauce. Cook for 1 to 2 minutes or until they are heated through.

Turn the roe mixture on to the toast slices, set on warmed plates, and serve.

Kipper Kedgeree

Kipper Kedgeree makes a delicious treat for Sunday breakfast. Alternatively, it may be served as an economical supper or lunch dish, accompanied by a tossed mixed salad and lots of brown bread and butter.

4 SERVINGS

1 lb. boned kipper fillets, skinned
2 oz. [¼ cup] butter
8 oz. [3 cups] cooked long-grain rice
2 fl. oz. double cream [¼ cup heavy cream]
4 hard-boiled eggs, finely chopped
¼ teaspoon salt
½ teaspoon freshly ground black pepper
1 teaspoon prepared English mustard

With a sharp knife, cut the kipper fillets into small pieces.

In a large deep frying-pan, melt the butter over moderate heat. When the foam subsides, add the kipper pieces and fry them for 3 to 4 minutes, turning them frequently, or until they are lightly browned.

Add the rice and stir in the cream and chopped eggs. Add the salt, pepper and mustard and cook, stirring constantly, for 3 minutes or until the mixture is heated through.

Remove the pan from the heat and turn the kedgeree into a large warmed serving dish.

Serve at once.

Kipper Paste

This traditional teatime treat is very popular with children. Serve the paste on thickly buttered toast on a cold winter's day. Once the paste has been made and potted, it should be eaten within 2 days.

12 OUNCES PASTE

4 oz. [2 cups] fresh white breadcrumbs
6 fl. oz. [¾ cup] water
4 kippers, cooked, skinned, filleted and flaked
1 garlic clove, crushed
2 oz. [¼ cup] butter, melted
juice of ½ lemon
½ teaspoon freshly ground black pepper
½ teaspoon cayenne pepper

Place the breadcrumbs in a mixing bowl and pour over the water. When the breadcrumbs are thoroughly soaked, squeeze out all the excess water.

This superb Kipper Paste was specially invented to be spread thickly on hot buttered toast!

Place the breadcrumbs, kippers, garlic, butter, lemon juice, pepper and cayenne in a mortar and pound them with a pestle until they form a smooth paste. Alternatively, blend all the ingredients in an electric blender until the paste is very smooth.

Spoon the paste into small pots. Cover the pots with aluminium foil and place in the refrigerator until required.

Kipper Pie

Covered with a golden pastry crust, this tasty Kipper Pie is delicious hot for supper with mashed potatoes and a fresh green vegetable, or cold, with lots of tossed mixed salad.

4 SERVINGS

1 oz. [2 tablespoons] butter
2 tablespoons flour
8 fl. oz. single cream [1 cup light cream]
12 oz. boned kipper fillets, poached, skinned and flaked
¼ teaspoon cayenne pepper
¼ teaspoon salt
½ teaspoon finely grated lemon rind
2 hard-boiled eggs, very thinly sliced
PASTRY
6 oz. [1½ cups] flour
⅛ teaspoon salt

Cool, refreshing Ceviche is an exotic blend of mackerel fillets marinated in lemon juice.

5 oz. [⅝ cup] butter, cut into walnut-sized pieces
3 to 4 tablespoons iced water
1 egg, lightly beaten

In a medium-sized saucepan, melt the butter over moderate heat. Remove the pan from the heat and, with a wooden spoon, stir in the flour to make a smooth paste. Gradually add the cream, stirring constantly. Return the pan to the heat and add the flaked kipper, cayenne, salt and lemon rind. Cook, stirring constantly, for 3 minutes, or until the mixture begins to boil.

Remove the pan from the heat and turn the mixture into a medium-sized pie dish. Carefully arrange the egg slices on top of the mixture. Set aside while you prepare the pastry.

Sift the flour and salt into a medium-sized mixing bowl. Add the butter and iced water. With a knife, mix quickly to a firm dough which should be lumpy.

On a lightly floured surface, roll out the dough into an oblong shape. Fold it in three and turn it so that the open edges face you. Roll out again into an oblong shape and proceed as before. Repeat this process once again to make three turns in all.

Wrap the dough in greaseproof or waxed paper and put it in the refrigerator to chill for 30 minutes.

Preheat the oven to fairly hot 400°F (Gas Mark 6, 200°C).

Remove the dough from the refrigerator. If it looks streaky, roll it out into an oblong shape and fold it in three once again. On a floured surface, roll out the dough to a circle 1-inch larger than the top of the pie dish. With a knife, cut a ½-inch strip around the dough. Dampen the rim of the dish with water and press the dough strip on to the rim. With a pastry brush dipped in water, lightly moisten the strip.

Using the rolling pin, lift the dough on to the dish. With a knife, trim the dough and, with your fingers, crimp the edges to seal them to the strip already on the dish. With a sharp knife, cut a 1-inch slit in the centre of the dough. With a pastry brush, coat the surface of the dough with the beaten egg.

Place the pie in the centre of the oven and bake for 50 minutes to 1 hour, or until the pastry is a deep golden brown.

Remove the pie from the oven and serve it at once, or set it aside and serve cold.

Ceviche

MACKEREL FILLETS MARINATED IN LEMON JUICE

This is a traditional Mexican dish, although it is also made in most South American countries with slight variations. The original recipe uses fresh limes but, if these are very difficult to obtain, Ceviche may also be made with fresh lemon juice. If you do use limes, use 8 fluid ounces [1 cup] of lime juice and 8 fluid ounces [1 cup] of lemon juice. Ceviche makes an unusual and delicious hors d'oeuvre or snack meal, accompanied by lots of brown bread and butter.

6 SERVINGS

16 fl. oz. [2 cups] fresh lemon juice
1 teaspoon dried, seeded, hot red chilli pepper, pounded in a mortar
2 medium-sized onions, very thinly sliced and pushed out into rings
½ garlic clove, finely chopped
1 teaspoon salt
½ teaspoon freshly ground black pepper
3 large mackerel, filleted and cut into 1-inch pieces
3 medium-sized sweet potatoes, unpeeled
2 crisp lettuces, washed, separated and chilled
4 ears fresh sweet corn, with outer husks and threads removed and cut across into 2-inch rounds
1 fresh red chilli, washed, split, seeded and cut into very thin pieces

Combine the lemon juice, pounded dried chilli pepper, onion rings, garlic, salt and pepper in a pitcher.

Place the fish pieces in a shallow porcelain dish and pour the lemon juice mixture over them. If the liquid does not cover the fish, add more lemon juice.

Cover the dish with aluminium foil and place it in the refrigerator. Leave the fish for at least 3 hours, or until it is opaque and white.

Thirty minutes before you are ready to serve the dish, bring 3 pints of water to the boil in a large saucepan over high heat. Place the sweet potatoes in the boiling water and cover the pan. Reduce the heat to moderate and cook for about 25 minutes, or until the potatoes are tender when pierced with the point of a sharp knife.

While the potatoes are cooking, arrange a bed of lettuce leaves on 6 individual plates. Set the plates aside.

Remove the pan from the heat and drain the potatoes in a colander. Peel the potatoes and cut each one into 3 slices. Keep the potato slices warm while you cook the corn.

In a medium-sized saucepan, bring 2 pints of water to the boil over high heat. Drop the corn rounds into the boiling water, reduce the heat to moderate and boil them for 4 to 5 minutes, or until the corn turns bright yellow.

Remove the pan from the heat and drain the corn in a colander.

Remove the marinated fish from the refrigerator. Using a slotted spoon, divide the fish between the six plates. Garnish the fish with the onion rings and strips of fresh chilli pepper.

Arrange the sweet potato slices and corn rounds round the fish and serve at once.

Mackerel Kebabs

Mackerel Kebabs are an unusual and tempting way of serving fish. They look especially attractive if served on a bed of watercress and garnished with black olives and slices of lemon.

4 SERVINGS

4 mackerel, cleaned, gutted and with backbones removed
6 pickling (pearl) onions
4 small tomatoes
4 button mushrooms, wiped clean
1 large green pepper, white pith removed, seeded and cut into ½-inch wide strips
2 fl. oz. [¼ cup] white wine vinegar
2 fl. oz. [¼ cup] olive oil
½ teaspoon salt
¼ teaspoon black pepper
1 teaspoon dried oregano

Cut each mackerel into 4 or 5 slices.

Thread the slices of fish on to skewers, alternating with the onions, tomatoes, mushrooms and green pepper strips.

In a large shallow dish, combine the vinegar, olive oil, salt, pepper and oregano. Lay the prepared skewers in the dish and leave to marinate at room temperature for about 2 hours, turning occasionally.

Preheat the grill [broiler] to high.

Remove the kebabs from the marinade and place them under the grill [broiler]. Cook for 8 to 10 minutes, basting the kebabs with the marinade and turning them frequently, or until the fish flakes easily when tested with a fork.

Serve the kebabs immediately, on a warmed serving dish.

12

A fish dish with a difference - Mackerel Kebabs may be served as an elegant first course for dinner or, on a bed of plain boiled rice, for a sustaining family lunch or supper.

Plaice [Flounder] with Artichoke Sauce

Plaice [flounder] fillets, simmered in court bouillon and served with a creamy artichoke sauce, is quick and easy to prepare and tastes delicious. Serve with steamed broccoli or peas, mashed potatoes and, to drink, some light white Burgundy wine, such as Pouilly Fuissé.

6 SERVINGS

2 lb. plaice [flounder] fillets
½ teaspoon salt
¼ teaspoon freshly ground black pepper
1 medium-sized onion, thinly sliced and pushed out into rings
1 celery stalk, trimmed and chopped
1 mace blade
bouquet garni, consisting of 4 parsley sprigs, 1 thyme spray and 1 bay leaf tied together
6 white peppercorns, finely crushed
10 fl. oz. [1¼ cups] home-made fish stock
6 fl. oz. [¾ cup] dry white wine or water
1 tablespoon lemon juice
1 tablespoon finely chopped fresh parsley
SAUCE
1 oz. [2 tablespoons] butter
1 oz. [¼ cup] flour
¼ teaspoon salt
⅛ teaspoon freshly ground black pepper
⅛ teaspoon cayenne pepper
2 fl. oz. double cream [¼ cup heavy cream]
3 artichoke hearts, simmered in boiling water for 35 minutes, drained and chopped

Put the plaice [flounder] fillets on a working surface and rub them all over with the salt and pepper. Lay the fillets, in one layer if possible, on the bottom of a large flameproof casserole. Add the onion rings, chopped celery, mace blade, bouquet garni and the white peppercorns. Pour over the stock and wine or water and add the lemon juice.

Place the casserole over moderately high heat and bring the liquid to the boil. Reduce the heat to moderately low, cover the casserole and cook for 12 to 15 minutes, or until the fish flakes easily when tested with a fork.

Remove the casserole from the heat.

Using a slotted spoon, carefully transfer the fish to a large warmed serving dish. Set aside and keep hot while you make the sauce.

Pour 10 fluid ounces [1¼ cups] of the cooking liquid through a fine wire strainer set over a medium-sized mixing bowl. Discard the contents of the strainer and set the bowl aside.

In a large frying-pan, melt the butter over moderate heat. Remove the pan from the heat and, with a wooden spoon, stir in the flour to make a smooth paste. Gradually add the strained cooking liquid, stirring constantly. Return the pan to the heat and cook, stirring constantly with a wooden spoon, for 2 to 3 minutes, or until the sauce is thick and smooth and hot but not boiling.

Remove the pan from the heat. Stir in the salt, pepper and cayenne. Stir in the cream, and then the artichoke heart pieces. Taste the sauce for seasoning and add more salt and pepper if necessary. Pour the sauce over the fish fillets and sprinkle them with the chopped fresh parsley.

Serve at once.

Plaice [flounder] is an under-used fish, but we guarantee that you'll want to cook it again and again once you've tasted rich, creamy Plaice [Flounder] with Artichoke Sauce!

Deep-Fried Whitebait

This is a basic recipe for whitebait. Serve with French-fried potatoes, lots of tossed mixed salad and some beer for a tasty light meal.

4 SERVINGS

2 oz. [½ cup] seasoned flour, made with 2 oz. [½ cup] flour, ½ teaspoon salt, ¼ teaspoon freshly ground black pepper and 1 tablespoon very finely chopped fresh parsley
1 lb. whitebait, rinsed and dried on kitchen paper towels sufficient vegetable oil for deep-frying

Place the seasoned flour on a large plate. Roll the whitebait in the seasoned flour, coating them thoroughly and shaking off any excess. Set aside.

Fill a large, deep-frying pan one-third full with vegetable oil and set it over moderate heat. Heat the oil until it reaches 360°F on a deep-fat thermometer or until a small cube of stale bread dropped into the oil turns golden in 50 seconds. Carefully place the whitebait in the oil and fry them, a handful at a time, for 2 to 3

minutes or until they are crisp and light brown. (If the whitebait stick together during frying, shake the pan gently from time to time.) Using a slotted spoon, transfer the whitebait to kitchen paper towels to drain. Keep hot while you cook and drain the remaining whitebait in the same way.

When all of the fish are cooked, carefully transfer the whitebait to a warmed serving dish and serve at once.

Whiting with Cheese and Breadcrumbs

A simple and relatively economical dish, Whiting with Cheese and Breadcrumbs is perfect for a family supper served with boiled potatoes and fresh minted peas or green beans. For special occasions, accompany this dish by some well-chilled Rhine wine, such as Liebfraumilch.

4 SERVINGS

4 medium-sized whiting fillets, skinned
1 teaspoon salt
½ teaspoon freshly ground black pepper
3 oz. [⅜ cup] butter

1 oz. [¼ cup] flour
8 fl. oz. [1 cup] milk
5 fl. oz. single cream [⅝ cup light cream]
6 oz. [1½ cups] Cheddar cheese, grated
2 oz. [⅔ cup] fine dry white breadcrumbs

Rub the fish all over with the salt and pepper. Set aside.

In a large frying-pan, melt 2 ounces [¼ cup] of the butter over moderate heat. When the foam subsides, add the fish and fry for 5 minutes on each side. Remove the pan from the heat and, using a fish slice or spatula, transfer the fish to a large warmed, flameproof serving dish. Set aside and keep hot while you prepare the sauce.

In a small saucepan, melt the remaining butter over moderate heat. Remove the pan from the heat and, using a wooden spoon, stir in the flour to form a

Deep-Fried Whitebait are easy to make, tasty to eat and economical to buy - serve them with French-fried potatoes and a tossed green salad for a simple but very satisfying meal.

smooth paste. Gradually add the milk and cream, stirring constantly and being careful to avoid lumps. Return the pan to the heat and cook the sauce, stirring constantly with a wooden spoon, for 2 to 3 minutes or until it is smooth and fairly thick and hot but not boiling. Remove the pan from the heat and pour the sauce over the fish.

Preheat the grill [broiler] to moderately high. Sprinkle the cheese and breadcrumbs over the fish. Place the dish under the grill [broiler] and grill [broil] for 3 to 5 minutes or until the top is golden brown and bubbling. Remove the flameproof serving dish from under the grill [broiler].

Serve immediately, straight from the dish.

Whiting Stuffed with Shrimps or Prawns

Whiting Stuffed with Shrimps or Prawns is a delicately flavoured French dish, ideal for lunch or dinner. Serve with croquette potatoes and creamed cauliflower or leeks, and a well-chilled white Burgundy wine such as Puligny-Montrachet or a slightly flinty Loire wine, such as Sancerre.

When you buy the whiting, ask the fish-

monger to remove the head, slit the fish open and bone and clean it.

6 SERVINGS

- 6 medium-sized whiting, boned and cleaned
- 1 lemon, quartered
- 1½ teaspoons salt
- 1 teaspoon freshly ground black pepper
- 4 oz. [½ cup] butter
- 10 oz. medium-sized button mushrooms, wiped clean and thinly sliced
- 10 oz. frozen and thawed shrimps or prawns, shelled
- 6 tablespoons finely chopped fresh parsley

Preheat the oven to moderate 350°F (Gas Mark 4, 180°C).

Wash the whiting under cold running water and pat them dry with kitchen paper towels. Squeeze the lemon quarters over the fish and discard the lemon. Rub the fish, inside and out, with 1 teaspoon of the salt and ½ teaspoon of the black pepper. Set the fish aside while you make the stuffing.

In a medium-sized frying-pan, melt 1 ounce [2 tablespoons] of the butter over moderate heat. When the foam subsides, add the sliced mushrooms and the remaining salt and pepper. Fry, stirring

Whiting Stuffed with Shrimps or Prawns is elegant enough to be served at the finest dinner party, inexpensive enough to be served as a sustaining family supper or dinner.

constantly, for 2 to 3 minutes, or until the mushrooms are just tender. Stir in the shrimps or prawns and parsley and cook the mixture, stirring and turning from time to time, for 2 to 3 minutes, or until the shrimps or prawns are thoroughly heated through.

Remove the pan from the heat. With a slotted spoon, remove the prawns or shrimps and mushrooms from the pan and stuff them carefully into the cavities of the fish.

With a sharp knife, cut half the remaining butter into small pieces and dot them over the bottom of a large, shallow baking dish. Place the stuffed fish, side by side, in the prepared dish, in one layer. Cut the remaining butter into small pieces and carefully scatter the pieces all over the fish.

Place the dish in the centre of the oven and bake for 20 to 30 minutes, or until the fish flakes easily when tested with a fork.

Remove the dish from the oven and serve immediately.

Jellied Fish Mould

A striking centrepiece for a summer buffet, Jellied Fish Mould is surprisingly quick and easy to make. Any fish may be used, but cod, haddock or salmon would be especially good.

6 SERVINGS

2 lb. cooked fish, skinned, boned and flaked
½ teaspoon salt
¼ teaspoon black pepper
2 tablespoons chopped fresh chives
1 oz. gelatine
4 fl. oz. [½ cup] hot fish stock
1 crisp lettuce, washed and shredded
8 stuffed olives, sliced

MAYONNAISE

1 egg yolk
¼ teaspoon salt
1 teaspoon paprika
1 teaspoon prepared mustard
5 fl. oz [⅝ cup] olive oil
2 to 3 teaspoons white wine vinegar or lemon juice
5 fl. oz. [⅝ cup] sour cream

First make the mayonnaise. Place the egg yolk, salt, paprika and mustard in a small mixing bowl. Using a wooden spoon, beat the ingredients until they are thoroughly blended.

Add the oil, a few drops at a time, beating constantly. After the mayonnaise has thickened, the oil may be added a little more rapidly. When all the oil has been added stir in the vinegar or lemon juice and the sour cream.

In a medium-sized mixing bowl, combine the fish, salt, pepper and chives. Beat in the mayonnaise.

In a small mixing bowl, dissolve the gelatine in the fish stock, stirring constantly.

Stir the dissolved gelatine into the fish mixture.

Rinse out a fish or ring mould with cold water and pour the fish mixture into the mould.

Leave the mould in the refrigerator for 2 hours, or until it is set.

To turn the mould out, quickly dip the base of the mould in hot water and turn it out on to a flat serving dish.

Surround the mould with the shredded lettuce and arrange the sliced stuffed olives on top.

Serve at once.

Mixed Fish Casserole

A filling spicy supper dish of Latin American origin, Mixed Fish Casserole may be served hot with a green vegetable and boiled potatoes, or left to cool and served with a salad. Accompany this dish with lots of well-chilled lager or some well-chilled Chilean white wine.

4-6 SERVINGS

2 fl. oz. [¼ cup] olive oil
6 medium-sized onions, finely chopped
3 medium-sized garlic cloves, crushed
1 large green pepper, white pith removed, seeded and cut into strips
1 large red pepper, white pith removed, seeded and cut into strips
1 tablespoon chopped fresh basil or 1½ teaspoons dried basil
1 lb. tomatoes, blanched, peeled

Jellied Fish Mould makes an excitingly different summer lunch or supper for the family.

and sliced
¼ teaspoon hot chilli powder
¼ teaspoon ground cumin
8 oz. halibut steaks, skinned
2 medium-sized mackerel fillets, skinned
8 oz. cod steaks, skinned
½ teaspoon salt
¼ teaspoon freshly ground black pepper
1 tablespoon white wine vinegar

In a large, flameproof casserole, heat the olive oil over moderate heat. When the oil is hot, add the onions and garlic and cook, stirring occasionally, for 5 to 7 minutes, or until the onions are soft and translucent but not brown.

Add the peppers, basil, tomatoes, chilli powder and cumin. Cover the casserole, reduce the heat to low and simmer the mixture for 1½ hours, or until it resembles a thick sauce.

Preheat the oven to warm 325°F (Gas Mark 3, 170°C).

Add the fish, salt and pepper to the casserole and stir well to mix. Place the casserole in the oven and bake for 20 to 30 minutes or until the fish flakes easily when tested with a fork.

Remove the casserole from the oven and stir in the vinegar. Serve immediately, or allow to cool before serving.

Seafood Stew

Seafood Stew should be served with boiled rice and a crisp green salad.

4 SERVINGS

8 fl. oz. [1 cup] dry white wine
1 lb. squid, cleaned thoroughly, skinned and cut into rings
1 tablespoon lemon juice
1 teaspoon salt
½ teaspoon black pepper
2 halibut steaks, bones removed
1 oz. [2 tablespoons] butter
1 tablespoon flour
½ teaspoon dried thyme
½ teaspoon dried rosemary
1 quart mussels, scrubbed, steamed and removed from their shells
8 oz. prawns or shrimps, shelled
2 oz. [½ cup] walnut halves
5 fl. oz. single cream [⅝ cup light cream]
2 tablespoons chopped parsley

Pour 4 fluid ounces [½ cup] of the white wine into a large saucepan. Add the squid, lemon juice, salt and pepper and bring the liquid to the boil over moderate heat. Reduce the heat to low and simmer for 30 minutes. Transfer the squid to a plate. Set aside.

Shrimps or prawns, mussels, halibut and squid combine in this delicately creamy Seafood Stew.

Add the halibut steaks and the remaining wine to the pan and cook the steaks for 5 to 8 minutes or until the flesh is almost tender. Transfer the halibut steaks to the plate. Set aside.

Pour the cooking liquid through a strainer into a bowl and set aside.

In a large flameproof casserole, melt the butter over moderate heat. Remove the casserole from the heat and, with a wooden spoon, stir in the flour to make a smooth paste. Pour the strained cooking liquid into the casserole, stirring constantly. Stir in the thyme and rosemary. Return the pan to moderate heat and bring the sauce to the boil, stirring constantly. Reduce the heat to low and simmer the sauce for 2 minutes.

Add the mussels, the reserved squid and halibut, the prawns or shrimps and walnuts to the sauce and cook for 7 to 10 minutes or until the halibut is tender and the mussels and prawns or shrimps are thoroughly heated through. Stir in the cream and cook the ragoût for a further 1 minute. Do not allow the sauce to boil. Remove the pan from the heat.

Sprinkle over the parsley and serve.

17

Halibut with Bananas

A delicious and unusual dish, Halibut with Bananas makes a very tasty lunch or dinner meal. Serve with creamed potatoes and cauliflower and accompany with a bottle of well-chilled Zeltinger white wine.

4 SERVINGS

3 oz. [1½ cups] fresh white breadcrumbs
1 egg, lightly beaten with 2 tablespoons milk, 1 teaspoon salt and ½ teaspoon white pepper
4 large halibut steaks
3 tablespoons vegetable oil
1 oz. [2 tablespoons] butter
2 oz. [½ cup] flaked almonds
3 tablespoons soft brown sugar
1 tablespoon fresh lemon juice
4 small bananas, peeled and halved lengthways

Place the breadcrumbs on one plate and the seasoned egg and milk mixture in another. Dip the fish steaks first in the egg and milk mixture, and then in the breadcrumbs, coating them thoroughly on both sides and shaking off any excess crumbs. Set the fish aside.

In a large, heavy frying-pan, heat the oil over moderate heat. When the oil is hot, add the fish and cook for 8 to 10 minutes on each side, or until the steaks are browned and flake easily when tested with a fork.

Remove the pan from the heat. Remove the fish steaks from the pan and arrange them on a warmed serving dish. Keep them hot.

Wipe out the frying-pan with kitchen paper towels. Return the pan to moderate heat and add the butter. When the foam subsides, add the flaked almonds and cook them, stirring frequently, for 3 minutes, or until they are lightly browned. Stir in the sugar, lemon juice and bananas and cook, turning the bananas once, for a further 3 minutes, or until the bananas are very tender but not mushy, and the sugar has formed a caramel syrup.

Remove the pan from the heat and arrange the banana mixture around the fish. Serve immediately.

Ocean Rolls

Ocean Rolls are fish fillets stuffed with shrimps or prawns, crabmeat, sweetcorn and dill, poached in white wine. Serve with duchess potatoes and peas for a super meal. For extra-special occasions, some well-chilled white wine would be an excellent accompaniment.

4 SERVINGS

4 white fish fillets, skinned
1 tablespoon lemon juice
1 tablespoon butter
1 shallot, finely chopped
4 oz. frozen and thawed shrimps or prawns, shelled
4 oz. canned or frozen crabmeat, drained or thawed
4 tablespoons canned drained sweetcorn kernels
½ teaspoon dried dill
½ teaspoon salt
½ teaspoon freshly ground black pepper
4 tablespoons double [heavy] cream
12 fl. oz. [1½ cups] dry white wine
1 bay leaf
1 small onion, sliced
1 tablespoon cornflour [cornstarch] mixed with 1 tablespoon white wine

Lay the fish fillets flat on a working surface and sprinkle them with the lemon juice. Set aside.

In a medium-sized frying-pan, melt the butter over moderate heat. When the foam subsides, add the shallot and fry, stirring constantly, for 3 to 4 minutes or until it is soft. Stir in the shrimps or prawns, crabmeat, sweetcorn, dill, salt, pepper and cream. Cook the mixture, stirring constantly, for 3 minutes.

Remove the pan from the heat. Spoon equal amounts of the mixture over each fish fillet. Spread it to the edges of the fillets with your fingertips. Roll up the fillets Swiss [jelly] roll style and secure the rolls with trussing thread or string. Set aside.

In a large, shallow saucepan, bring the wine, bay leaf and onion to the boil over moderately high heat. With a slotted spoon, lower the fish rolls into the liquid, arranging them in one layer. Reduce the heat to low and simmer for 10 minutes.

With the slotted spoon, carefully turn the fish rolls over. Simmer for a further 10 minutes, or until the fish flakes easily when tested with a fork.

Remove the pan from the heat. With the slotted spoon, lift the rolls out of the pan and transfer them to a warmed serving dish. Remove and discard the trussing thread or string. Set aside and keep warm while you finish the sauce.

With the slotted spoon, remove and discard the onion and bay leaf from the cooking liquid. Return the pan to the heat, increase the heat to high and bring the liquid to the boil. Boil for 5 minutes or until the liquid has reduced to one-third of the original quantity.

Reduce the heat to low. Stir in the cornflour [cornstarch] mixture until the sauce is thick and smooth.

Remove the pan from the heat. Pour the sauce over the fish rolls and serve immediately.

Sole Fillets with Tomatoes and Garlic

Quick and easy to make, Sole Fillets with Tomatoes and Garlic is a strongly flavoured dish. It makes an excellent main course accompanied by creamed potatoes and courgettes [zucchini]. Serve with a well chilled white Frascati wine.

4 SERVINGS

2 tablespoons olive oil
1 lb. tomatoes, blanched, peeled, seeded and chopped
4 oz. canned tomato purée
2 large garlic cloves, crushed
1 teaspoon dried oregano
1 teaspoon salt
¼ teaspoon freshly ground black pepper
3 tablespoons flour
2 soles, filleted
1 oz. [2 tablespoons] butter
12 large black olives, stoned

First make the sauce. In a medium-sized saucepan, heat the oil over high heat. Add the tomatoes, tomato purée, garlic, oregano, half the salt and the pepper. Stir to mix. Reduce the heat to low, cover the pan and simmer the sauce for 30 minutes or until it is thick and smooth. If necessary, remove the lid and cook the sauce uncovered, stirring occasionally, until it has the required consistency.

While the sauce is simmering, cook the fish. Mix the flour with the remaining salt on a large plate. Dip the sole fillets in the flour mixture and coat them thoroughly on both sides, shaking off any excess.

Preheat the oven to moderate 350°F (Gas Mark 4, 180°C).

In a large frying-pan, melt the butter over moderately high heat. When the foam subsides, add the fish fillets two at a time. Reduce the heat to moderate and fry the fish for 2 minutes on each side. Transfer the fillets to an ovenproof dish and keep them warm while you cook the remaining fillets in the same way.

When the sauce is ready, stir in the olives. Pour the sauce over the fish. Place the dish in the centre of the oven and bake for 20 minutes. Serve immediately.

Ocean Rolls are guaranteed to make special occasions more special!

Smoked Salmon Quiche

An elegant and easy-to-make dish, Smoked Salmon Quiche may be served as a first course for a dinner party or, with lots of mixed salad and crusty bread, as a light supper or lunch. Accompany it with a bottle of well-chilled Traminer wine.

4-6 SERVINGS

1 x 9-inch flan case made with shortcrust pastry
FILLING
4 oz. smoked salmon, cut into 2-inch pieces
4 fl. oz. single cream [½ cup light cream]
3 eggs
2 oz. [½ cup] Gruyère cheese, grated
¼ teaspoon white pepper

Preheat the oven to fairly hot 400°F (Gas Mark 6, 200°C). Place the flan case on a baking sheet.

Arrange the smoked salmon pieces over the bottom of the flan case and set aside.

In a medium-sized mixing bowl, combine the cream, eggs, grated cheese and pepper and beat well to blend. Pour the mixture over the smoked salmon and place the baking sheet in the oven. Bake the quiche for 25 to 30 minutes or until the filling is set and firm and golden brown on top.

Remove the baking sheet from the oven and serve the quiche at once if you are serving it hot.

Grilled [Broiled] Trout

A fragrant Italian way of cooking trout, Grilled [Broiled] Trout makes a sumptuous light lunch when served with fennel and stuffed tomatoes.

4 SERVINGS

4 medium-sized trout, cleaned and with the eyes removed
¼ teaspoon salt
½ teaspoon black pepper
2 garlic cloves, halved
4 rosemary sprays
3 tablespoons olive oil
1 lemon, cut into 8 wedges

Preheat the grill [broiler] to moderate.

Place the fish on a wooden board and rub them all over with the salt and pepper. Place half a garlic clove and 1 rosemary spray in the cavity of each fish. With a sharp knife, make 3 shallow cuts on each side of the fish and arrange the trout in the grill [broiler] pan.

With a pastry brush, lightly coat the trout with the oil. Grill [broil] the fish for

5 minutes. Remove the grill [broiler] pan from the heat and, using a fish slice or spatula, turn the fish over. Brush the fish with the remaining oil and return the pan to the heat. Grill [broil] for a further 5 to 6 minutes or until the fish flesh flakes easily when tested with a fork.

Transfer the trout to a warmed serving dish. Remove and discard the garlic and rosemary and garnish the fish with the lemon wedges. Serve immediately.

Tuna Steaks Provençal-Style

Tuna is even more delicious fresh than it is canned, and this superb recipe for Tuna Steaks Provençal-Style really does the fish justice. Serve the dish with sautéed courgettes [zucchini], potatoes and well-chilled white wine.

4 SERVINGS

4 tuna steaks, approximately ½-inch thick
½ teaspoon salt
½ teaspoon freshly ground black pepper
2 fl. oz. [¼ cup] olive oil
1 large onion, finely chopped
2 garlic cloves, crushed
14 oz. canned peeled tomatoes
8 black olives, stoned and chopped
MARINADE
3 fl. oz. [⅜ cup] olive oil
3 fl. oz. [⅜ cup] dry white wine
2 tablespoons lemon juice
2 garlic cloves, crushed
1 teaspoon freshly ground black pepper
1 teaspoon dried basil

First make the marinade. In a large, shallow dish, combine all the marinade ingredients, beating with a fork until they are well mixed. Add the tuna steaks to the dish and baste them well with the marinade. Set aside at room temperature for 2 hours, basting occasionally.

Remove the tuna steaks from the marinade and pat them dry with kitchen paper towels. Reserve the marinade.

Rub the salt and pepper into the tuna steaks and set them aside.

In a large, deep frying-pan, heat the olive oil over moderate heat. When the oil is hot, add the onion and garlic and fry, stirring frequently, for 5 to 7 minutes or until the onion is soft and translucent but not brown. Add the tomatoes with the can juice and olives and cook for a further 3 minutes.

Pour in the reserved marinade and bring the mixture to the boil. Reduce the heat to low and simmer the mixture, uncovered, for 20 minutes or until the

sauce is fairly thick.

Add the tuna steaks to the pan and cook for 8 to 10 minutes on each side, or until the fish flakes easily when tested with a fork. Remove the pan from the heat. Using a slotted spoon, transfer the fish to a warmed serving dish. Pour over the sauce and serve at once.

Yugoslavian Fish Steaks

A delicately flavoured, lightly spiced dish, Yugoslavian Fish Steaks is an unusual way to serve any firm, white-fleshed fish. The dish may be served with plain boiled rice

and spinach.

4 SERVINGS

- 2 oz. [4 tablespoons] butter
- 2 tablespoons vegetable oil
- 2 medium-sized onions, thinly sliced
- 1 lb. tomatoes, blanched, peeled, seeded and chopped or 14 oz. canned peeled tomatoes, drained
- 3 fl. oz. [⅜ cup] white wine
- 1 tablespoon white wine vinegar
- ¼ teaspoon cayenne pepper
- ¼ teaspoon freshly ground black pepper
- 1½ teaspoons salt
- ½ teaspoon dried tarragon
- 2 tablespoons flour

4 x 8 oz. steaks of any firm white fish

In a medium-sized saucepan, melt 1 ounce [2 tablespoons] of the butter and half of the oil over moderate heat. When the foam subsides, add the onions and fry them for 5 to 7 minutes. Add the tomatoes, wine, wine vinegar, cayenne, pepper, ½ teaspoon salt and tarragon. Bring the liquid to the boil, cover, reduce the heat to moderately low and simmer gently for 30 minutes, stirring occasionally.

While the sauce is simmering, combine the remaining salt and flour together on a plate. Dip the fish steaks in the mixture and coat them well on both sides.

Grilled [Broiled] Trout is a superbly easy way to cook an exceptionally tasty fish. Serve with stuffed tomatoes.

Ten minutes before the end of the sauce's cooking time, melt the remaining butter and oil in a large frying-pan over moderate heat. When the butter foam subsides, add the salted, floured fish to the pan. Cook for 5 to 6 minutes on each side, or until the steaks are lightly browned, adding more butter and oil if necessary. Transfer the fish steaks to a warmed serving dish and spoon the sauce over them. Serve at once.

21

Clams

Clam and Corn Bake

Clam and Corn Bake, made with clams, prawns or shrimps, sweetcorn and cream, with a cheese topping, is delicious served hot or cold with a tossed green salad.

4 SERVINGS

10 fl. oz. double cream [1¼ cups heavy cream]
3 eggs
½ teaspoon salt
¼ teaspoon black pepper
⅛ teaspoon cayenne pepper
1 tablespoon finely chopped fresh chives (optional)
10 oz. fresh, frozen or canned and drained sweetcorn
8 oz. prawns or shrimps, shelled
15 clams, steamed, removed from their shells and coarsely chopped
2 oz. [½ cup] Cheddar cheese, grated
1 oz. [¼ cup] dry breadcrumbs
1 oz. [2 tablespoons] butter

Preheat the oven to moderate 350°F (Gas Mark 4, 180°C).

In a medium-sized mixing bowl, using a wire whisk or rotary beater, lightly beat together the cream, eggs, salt, pepper and cayenne. Stir in the chives, if you are using them, the sweetcorn, prawns or shrimps and clams.

Turn the mixture out into a lightly greased soufflé dish and set aside.

In a small mixing bowl, combine the grated cheese and breadcrumbs and spoon this over the mixture in the soufflé dish. Cut the butter into small pieces and dot over the top.

Place the dish in the oven and bake for 1 hour or until the top is golden.

Remove the dish from the oven and serve immediately, or cool and serve cold.

Japanese Clams

Serve Japanese Clams as an hors d'oeuvre or as part of a Japanese meal.

4 SERVINGS

2 fl. oz. [¼ cup] sake
2 tablespoons sugar
12 clams, removed from their shells
2 tablespoons soy sauce

In a large, heavy frying-pan, combine the sake, sugar and clams. With a wooden spoon, stir the mixture thoroughly. Bring the mixture to the boil over high heat and boil it for 3 minutes, stirring constantly. Stir in the soy sauce and cook for 1 minute, still stirring. Remove the clams from the pan and set aside.

Continue boiling the sauce in the frying-pan for a further 10 minutes or until it becomes thick and syrupy. Return the clams to the pan and stir them gently into the sauce. Cook the mixture, stirring constantly, for 1 minute.

Remove from the heat and serve.

Stuffed Clams

Grilled [broiled] clams flavoured with garlic and parsley, Stuffed Clams may be served as a special hors d'oeuvre, on their own or garnished with lemon wedges, or as a

Clam and Corn Bake is an economical dish from the United States.

light lunch with lots of tomato salad and crusty bread.

4 SERVINGS

24 clams, scrubbed and steamed
3½ oz. [⅜ cup plus 1 tablespoon] butter, melted
2 oz. [⅔ cup] dry white breadcrumbs
2 garlic cloves, crushed
2 tablespoons finely chopped fresh parsley
½ teaspoon salt
½ teaspoon freshly ground black pepper
2 parsley sprigs

Remove and discard the upper clam shell halves, leaving the flesh in the bottom shell halves. Set the clams aside.

Preheat the grill [broiler] to moderately high.

In a small mixing bowl, combine the butter, breadcrumbs, garlic, chopped parsley, salt and pepper.

Sprinkle the mixture evenly over each clam, pressing the mixture down lightly over the clam flesh with your fingertips.

Place the clams, flesh sides up, in a large flameproof dish, in one layer if possible.

Place the dish under the grill [broiler] and grill [broil] the clams for 5 to 6 minutes, or until the topping is golden brown.

Remove the dish from the heat. Garnish with the parsley sprigs and serve immediately.

Clams Baked with Potatoes and Sweetcorn

Easy and quick to make, Clams Baked with Potatoes and Sweetcorn is an inexpensive dish, perfect for a light lunch or dinner.

4 SERVINGS

1 teaspoon butter
2 lb. potatoes, cooked and mashed
2 fl. oz. double cream [¼ cup heavy cream]
2 tablespoons tomato purée
2 teaspoons finely chopped fresh chives
1 teaspoon salt
½ teaspoon black pepper
¼ teaspoon dried thyme
¼ teaspoon grated nutmeg
¼ teaspoon cayenne pepper
1 garlic clove, crushed

These clams are stuffed with parsley, breadcrumbs and garlic.

1 lb. canned clams, drained
10 oz. canned sweetcorn, drained
4 oz. Bel Paese cheese, thinly sliced

Preheat the oven to fairly hot 400°F (Gas Mark 6, 200°C).

With the teaspoon of butter, grease a medium-sized, deep-sided baking dish and set it aside.

In a large mixing bowl, beat the mashed potatoes and cream together with a wooden spoon until the mixture is smooth. Beat in the tomato purée, chives, salt, pepper, thyme, nutmeg, cayenne and garlic. Stir in the clams and sweetcorn and combine the mixture thoroughly.

Spoon the mixture into the prepared baking dish and smooth it down with the back of the spoon. Lay the cheese slices over the mixture to cover it completely.

Place the dish in the centre of the oven and bake for 15 to 20 minutes, or until the cheese has melted and is golden brown.

Remove the dish from the oven and serve immediately.

Mussels Baked with Basil and Tomato Sauce

A delightful dish for a family supper, Mussels Baked with Basil and Tomato Sauce is easy to prepare and fairly economical. It may be served with buttered noodles and a crisp green salad.

4 SERVINGS

1 tablespoon plus 1 teaspoon butter
3 tablespoons olive oil
1 large onion, finely chopped
3 garlic cloves, crushed
1½ lb. canned peeled tomatoes, chopped
½ teaspoon salt
¼ teaspoon black pepper
3 tablespoons chopped fresh basil or 1½ tablespoons dried basil
3 quarts mussels, scrubbed, steamed and removed from their shells
2 tablespoons fresh breadcrumbs
2 oz. [½ cup] Parmesan cheese, grated

Preheat the oven to moderate 350°F (Gas Mark 4, 180°C).

With the teaspoon of butter, lightly grease a medium-sized baking dish.

In a medium-sized saucepan, melt the remaining butter with the olive oil over moderate heat. When the foam subsides, add the onion and garlic and cook, stirring occasionally, for 5 to 7 minutes, or until the onion is soft and translucent but not brown.

Stir in the tomatoes with the can juice, the salt, pepper and basil. Reduce the heat to low and simmer the sauce, stirring occasionally, for 15 minutes. Remove the pan from the heat and stir in the mussels. Pour the mixture into the prepared dish.

In a small bowl, combine the breadcrumbs and grated cheese, mixing until they are well blended. Sprinkle the mixture over the mussel mixture.

Place the dish in the centre of the oven and bake for 20 minutes, or until the top is golden brown and bubbling. Remove the dish from the oven and serve.

Mussel and Beef Pie

A traditional English recipe, Mussel and Beef Pie makes a wonderfully nourishing and sustaining meal.

6 SERVINGS

2 oz. [¼ cup] butter
2 tablespoons vegetable oil
2 lb. lean stewing beef, cut into 1-inch cubes
1 large onion, finely chopped
2 potatoes, peeled and diced
8 oz. mushrooms, wiped clean and sliced
8 fl. oz. [1 cup] dark beer
½ teaspoon dried thyme
½ teaspoon salt
¼ teaspoon black pepper
1 quart mussels, scrubbed, steamed and removed from their shells

PASTRY

6 oz. [1½ cups] flour
¼ teaspoon salt
4 oz. [½ cup] butter
3 to 4 tablespoons iced water
1 egg, lightly beaten

First make the pastry. Sift the flour and salt into a bowl. Cut the butter into small pieces and add them to the flour. Pour in the water and mix quickly into a dough, which should be lumpy.

On a floured surface, roll out the dough into an oblong shape. Fold it in three and turn it so that the open edges face you. Roll again into an oblong shape and fold and turn as before. Repeat once again to make three folds and turns in all. Chill the dough while you make the filling.

Preheat the oven to fairly hot 400°F (Gas Mark 6, 200°C).

Meanwhile, prepare the filling. In a large frying-pan, melt the butter with the oil over moderate heat. When the foam subsides, add the beef cubes, a few at a time, and cook, stirring and turning occasionally, for 8 to 10 minutes or until they are evenly browned. Transfer the cubes to a plate and keep warm while you brown the remaining meat in the same way.

Add the onion and potatoes to the pan and cook, stirring occasionally, for 5 to 7 minutes or until the onion is soft and translucent but not brown. Stir in the mushrooms and cook the mixture for a further 3 minutes.

Pour over the beer and add the thyme, salt and pepper, mixing well to blend. Increase the heat to high and bring the mixture to the boil. Reduce the heat to moderate and return the beef cubes to the pan, stirring well to mix. Simmer the mixture for 15 minutes.

Stir in the mussels and remove the pan from the heat. Pour the mixture into a 9-inch pie dish and set aside.

Remove the dough from the refrigerator. If it looks streaky, roll it out into an oblong shape and fold it in three once again. Roll it out to a piece 1-inch larger than the top of the pie dish. With a sharp knife, cut a ½-inch strip around the dough. Dampen the rim of the dish with water and press the dough strip on to the rim. With a pastry brush dipped in water, lightly moisten the strip.

Using the rolling pin, lift the dough on to the dish. With a knife, trim the dough and, with your fingers, crimp the edges to seal them to the strip already on the dish. With a sharp knife, cut a cross in the centre of the dough. With a pastry brush, coat the surface with the beaten egg.

Place the pie in the oven and bake for 45 to 50 minutes or until the pastry is golden brown.

Remove the pie from the oven and serve.

Mussels with Lemon Sauce

Mussels with Lemon Sauce have a fresh tangy flavour and make a delicious main course for a summer meal.

4 SERVINGS

2½ quarts mussels
2 oz. [¼ cup] butter

2 shallots, finely chopped
  bouquet garni consisting of 4
  parsley sprigs, 1 thyme spray
  and 1 bay leaf tied together
½ teaspoon salt
½ teaspoon black pepper
¼ teaspoon grated nutmeg
  juice of 4 lemons
1 tablespoon flour

Wash the mussels in cold water and, with a stiff brush, scrub them to remove any mud on their shells. Discard any mussels which are not tightly shut or do not close if sharply tapped, and any that float or have broken shells. With a sharp knife, scrape off the tufts of hair, or beards, which protrude from between the closed shell halves. Place the mussels in a large bowl of cold water and soak them for 1 hour. Drain the mussels in a colander and set aside.

In a large saucepan, melt half the butter over moderate heat. When the foam subsides, add the shallots, bouquet garni, salt, pepper and nutmeg. Cook, stirring occasionally, for 2 to 3 minutes, or until the shallots are soft and translucent but not brown. Stir in the lemon juice.

Increase the heat to moderately high and add the mussels to the pan. Cook the mussels, shaking the pan constantly, for 3 minutes or until the shells open.

Remove the pan from the heat. Transfer the mussels and cooking liquid to a large strainer set over a large bowl. Reserve the strained liquid. Set the mussels aside and keep warm.

In a small saucepan, melt the remaining butter over moderate heat. Remove the pan from the heat and, with a wooden spoon, stir in the flour to make a smooth paste. Gradually add the reserved strained cooking liquid, stirring constantly. Return the pan to low heat and, stirring constantly, cook the sauce for 3 to 4 minutes or until it is thick and smooth. Remove the pan from the heat.

Arrange the mussels decoratively in a large warmed serving dish and pour the sauce over them. Serve immediately.

Mussels Mariners' Style

Mussels Mariners' Style make an excellent first course, served in deep soup bowls with a fork to eat the mussels and a soup spoon for the juices.

4 SERVINGS

3 quarts mussels
2 oz. [¼ cup] butter
1 small onion, finely chopped
1 garlic clove, crushed
1 celery stalk, trimmed and finely
  chopped
  bouquet garni consisting of 4
  parsley sprigs, 1 thyme spray
  and 1 bay leaf tied together
16 fl. oz. [2 cups] dry white wine
½ teaspoon salt
¼ teaspoon black pepper
2 tablespoons chopped parsley

Wash the mussels in cold water and, with a stiff brush, scrub them to remove any mud on their shells. Discard any mussels which are not tightly shut or do not close if sharply tapped, and any that float or have broken shells.

With a sharp knife, scrape off the tufts of hair, or beards, which protrude from between the closed shell halves. Place the mussels in a large bowl of cold water and soak them for 1 hour. Drain the mussels in a colander and set aside.

In a large saucepan, melt the butter over moderate heat. When the foam subsides, add the onion and garlic and fry, stirring occasionally, for 5 to 7 minutes or until the onion is soft and translucent but not brown. Add the celery, bouquet garni, wine, salt and pepper and bring the mixture to the boil. Reduce the heat to low, add the mussels and simmer, shaking the pan occasionally, for 5 to 10 minutes, or until the shells open. With a slotted spoon, transfer the mussels to a warmed serving dish. Remove and discard the empty shell halves from the mussels.

Strain the mussel cooking liquid into a bowl, then return it to the saucepan. Place the pan over high heat and bring it to the boil. Boil for 2 minutes. Pour the liquid over the mussels, sprinkle over the parsley and serve.

Mussels Baked with Basil and Tomato Sauce.

25

Prawns or Shrimps

Chinese Deep-Fried Prawns

Chinese Deep-Fried Prawns may be served as part of a complete Chinese meal.

4-6 SERVINGS

3 tablespoons tomato purée
2 tablespoons soy sauce
1 teaspoon chilli sauce
1 teaspoon sugar
1½ lb. large prawns or shrimps
1 egg, lightly beaten
3 tablespoons flour
2 teaspoons cornflour [cornstarch]
1 slice root ginger, very finely diced
½ teaspoon salt
3 fl. oz. [⅜ cup] water
sufficient oil for deep-frying

In a small bowl mix together the tomato purée, soy sauce, chilli sauce and sugar until they are thoroughly blended. Put this sauce in a sauceboat and set aside.

To prepare the prawns for cooking, remove the shells leaving the tail shell intact. Under cold running water, remove the black veins from the back flesh. Drain.

To make the batter, put the beaten egg into a medium-sized bowl and, beating continuously with a wire whisk, add the flour, cornflour [cornstarch], ginger, salt and water. Beat until the batter is smooth.

In a deep-frying pan, heat the oil over high heat until it registers 350°F on a deep-fat thermometer, or until a small cube of dry bread dropped into the oil turns golden brown in 55 seconds.

Holding the prawns by the tail, dip each one in the batter. As soon as the oil reaches the correct temperature, put the prawns in a deep-frying basket and put the basket in the oil. Fry the prawns for 2 to 3 minutes, or until they become golden brown. Remove the deep-frying basket from the oil and drain the prawns.

Arrange the prawns on a heated serving dish and serve them with the sauce.

Prawn or Shrimp Cocktail

A very popular first course, Prawn or Shrimp Cocktail is simple to prepare.

4 SERVINGS

4 large lettuce leaves, washed, shaken dry and shredded
6 fl. oz. [¾ cup] mayonnaise
4 tablespoons double [heavy] cream
2 teaspoons Worcestershire sauce
2 teaspoons lemon juice
2 teaspoons tomato ketchup
¼ teaspoon cayenne pepper
½ teaspoon salt
½ teaspoon black pepper
14 oz. prawns or shrimps, shelled
1 teaspoon paprika
4 thin cucumber slices
1 lemon, quartered

Stand 4 individual serving glasses on 4 small plates. Divide the shredded lettuce equally among the glasses and set aside.

In a medium-sized mixing bowl, combine the mayonnaise, cream, Worcestershire sauce, lemon juice, tomato ketchup, cayenne, salt and pepper, beating with a wooden spoon until the mixture is smooth. Stir in the prawns or shrimps.

Spoon the mixture equally over the lettuce and sprinkle over the paprika.

Garnish with the cucumber and lemon quarters and serve immediately.

Creole Shrimps

Serve this tasty dish with plain boiled rice and a mixed salad.

4 SERVINGS

2 tablespoons olive oil
2 celery stalks, finely chopped

Exotic Chinese Deep-Fried Prawns.

2 large onions, finely chopped
8 fl. oz. [1 cup] dry white wine
14 oz. canned peeled tomatoes, drained and roughly chopped
1 teaspoon salt
1 tablespoon red wine vinegar
1 tablespoon sugar
1 green pepper, white pith removed, seeded and chopped
1 tablespoon cornflour [cornstarch], mixed with 2 fl. oz. [¼ cup] water
1½ lb. frozen shelled shrimps, thawed

In a large, deep frying-pan, heat the oil over moderate heat. Add the celery and onions and fry for 5 to 7 minutes, or until the onions are soft and transparent.

Pour the wine into the pan, reduce the heat to low and simmer for 10 minutes, stirring occasionally.

Add the tomatoes, salt, vinegar and sugar to the pan. Continue simmering for a further 10 minutes, stirring occasionally.

Add the green pepper to the pan and simmer for 10 minutes.

Stir in the cornflour [cornstarch] mixture. Raise the heat to moderate, bring the sauce to the boil and cook for 3 minutes.

Add the shrimps to the pan and cook for 4 to 5 minutes longer to heat them through. Remove the pan from the heat and spoon the shrimp mixture on to a bed of rice. Serve immediately.

Prawn or Shrimp and Crabmeat Spread

☆   ① ①   ⋈ ⋈

Prawn or Shrimp and Crabmeat Spread makes an excellent first course, served on thin triangles of toast.

12 OUNCES [1½ CUPS]

4 oz. cooked crabmeat, fresh or canned, shell and cartilage removed

Serve traditional Creole Shrimps on a bed of plain boiled rice.

2 oz. [¼ cup] butter, softened
2 tablespoons double [heavy] cream
⅛ teaspoon cayenne pepper
¼ teaspoon salt
1 teaspoon fresh lemon juice
8 oz. frozen prawns or shrimps, thawed and shelled

Place the crabmeat, butter and cream in a mortar. Using a pestle, pound the mixture until it is smooth. Alternatively, place the ingredients in an electric blender and blend, on and off, for 30 seconds.

Spoon the mixture into a medium-sized mixing bowl. Using a fork, mash in the cayenne, salt and lemon juice. Mix in the prawns or shrimps.

Cover the bowl and chill it in the refrigerator for 1 hour before serving.

Prawn or Shrimp Curry

This is a strong curry flavoured with coconut, from South India. If coconuts are not available make the coconut milk with 4 ounces of creamed coconut and 12 fluid ounces [1½ cups] of boiling water.

4-6 SERVINGS

1½-inch piece fresh root ginger, peeled and chopped
3 garlic cloves
4 green chillis, seeded
6 tablespoons chopped fresh coriander leaves (1 bunch)
1 tablespoon whole coriander seeds
juice of 1 lemon
15 fl. oz. [1⅞ cups] thick coconut milk
6 tablespoons vegetable oil
1½ lb. large prawns or shrimps, shelled
2 medium-sized onions, finely chopped
1 teaspoon turmeric
1 teaspoon mustard seed
1 teaspoon salt

Put the ginger, garlic, chillis, coriander leaves and seeds, and the lemon juice in the jar of an electric blender. Pour in 4 tablespoons of the coconut milk. Blend at high speed until the mixture forms a thick paste. Add more coconut milk if the blender sticks. Scrape out the paste and set it aside in a small mixing bowl.

In a large saucepan, heat 4 tablespoons of the oil over moderate heat. When the oil is hot, add the prawns or shrimps and

Potted Shrimps or Prawns is an all-time British favourite.

fry them, turning them frequently, for 5 minutes. With a slotted spoon, transfer the prawns or shrimps to a plate. Set aside.

Add the remaining oil to the pan. When the oil is hot, add the onions and fry them, stirring occasionally, for 8 to 10 minutes or until they are golden brown. Add the turmeric, mustard seed and salt and fry, stirring constantly, for 1 minute. Add the spice paste and fry, stirring constantly, for 5 minutes. Add the prawns or shrimps and remaining coconut milk and cook for 1 minute. When the curry boils, cover the pan, reduce the heat to low and simmer for 30 minutes. Taste the curry and add more salt or lemon juice if necessary.

Remove the pan from the heat. Spoon the curry into a heated serving bowl. Serve immediately.

Greek Prawns or Shrimps with Tomato Sauce

A traditional Greek dish, Greek Prawns or Shrimps with Tomato Sauce is simple to prepare and makes an appetizing and light luncheon dish. Serve with rice and a mixed green salad and a well-chilled Greek white wine, such as Hymmetus.

4-6 SERVINGS

2 oz. [¼ cup] butter
1 medium-sized onion, thinly sliced
2 garlic cloves, crushed
2 lb. fresh tomatoes, blanched peeled, seeded and chopped, or 2 lb. canned peeled tomatoes, drained and chopped
1 teaspoon sugar
1 teaspoon chopped fresh oregano or ½ teaspoon dried oregano
1 teaspoon chopped fresh basil or ½ teaspoon dried basil
1 bay leaf
1 tablespoon chopped fresh parsley
8 fl. oz. [1 cup] dry white wine
1 teaspoon salt
½ teaspoon freshly ground black pepper
1 lb. frozen Dublin Bay prawns [large Gulf shrimps], thawed and shelled
3 oz. feta cheese, cut into small cubes

In a large, heavy frying-pan, melt the butter over moderate heat. When the foam subsides, add the onion and garlic to the pan and cook them, stirring occasionally, for 5 to 7 minutes, or until the onion is soft and translucent but not brown.

Add the tomatoes, sugar, oregano, basil, bay leaf and parsley to the pan and stir well to mix. Reduce the heat to low, cover the pan and simmer the sauce for 15 minutes, stirring occasionally.

Stir in the wine and increase the heat to high. Bring the liquid to the boil. Reduce the heat to low and simmer the sauce, uncovered, for a further 30 minutes, or until it has thickened and reduced somewhat.

Stir in the salt, pepper, prawns and cheese. Cook the mixture for 8 to 10 minutes, or until the prawns are heated through and the cheese has melted.

Remove the pan from the heat and remove and discard the bay leaf. Spoon the mixture into a warmed serving dish and serve at once.

Potted Shrimps or Prawns

A traditional British speciality, Potted Shrimps or Prawns are very easy to prepare. White fish is often added to the shrimps or prawns and the mixture may be put into one big dish rather than small individual pots. Serve with thin slices of brown bread and garnish with watercress. Potted Shrimps or Prawns may be kept for up to 1 week in the refrigerator.

10 SERVINGS

5 oz. [⅝ cup] butter
¼ teaspoon ground mace

⅛ teaspoon cayenne pepper
½ teaspoon salt
½ teaspoon black pepper
1 lb. shrimps or prawns, cooked
and shelled
5 oz. [⅝ cup] clarified butter, melted

In a large frying-pan, melt the butter over moderate heat. When the foam subsides, stir in the mace, cayenne, salt and pepper. Add the shrimps or prawns to the pan and coat them thoroughly with the seasoned butter. Remove the pan from the heat.

Spoon equal amounts of the mixture into 10 small pots, leaving a ¼-inch space at the top. Pour 1 tablespoon of the clarified butter into each pot. Cover the pots with aluminium foil and put them in the refrigerator to chill for at least 2 hours.

Remove the pots from the refrigerator. Remove and discard the foil and serve at once.

Prawn Savoury

A simple, quickly made dish suitable for lunch or supper, Prawn Savoury may be accompanied by a tomato salad and a baked potato with sour cream.

6 SERVINGS

2 oz. [4 tablespoons] butter
16 oz. canned and drained or frozen
and thawed corn kernels
1 green pepper, white pith removed,
seeded and finely chopped
12 oz. [1½ cups] cooked prawns or
shrimps, shelled
4 fl. oz. double cream [½ cup heavy
cream]
¼ teaspoon salt
¼ teaspoon black pepper
6 slices toast
⅛ teaspoon cayenne pepper

In a large, heavy frying-pan, melt the butter over moderate heat. Add the corn and green pepper to the pan and sauté them gently for 5 minutes, stirring occasionally. Add the prawns and cream and simmer the mixture for 4 more minutes, or until the prawns are thoroughly heated. Add the salt and pepper. Spoon the mixture on to the toast, sprinkle with the cayenne and serve immediately.

Scampi Kebabs

These unusual kebabs, made with prawns [shrimps], peppers and mushrooms and flavoured with lemon, garlic and sage, have a distinctly Mediterranean appearance.

4 SERVINGS

16 Dublin Bay prawns [large Gulf
shrimps], shelled
2 green peppers, white pith
removed, seeded and cut into 16
pieces
16 medium-sized mushrooms,
wiped clean and stalks removed
16 sage leaves
2 lemons, quartered and each
quarter cut across in half
MARINADE
2 fl. oz. [¼ cup] olive oil
2 tablespoons lemon juice
3 garlic cloves, crushed
1 teaspoon salt
¾ teaspoon black pepper

In a large, shallow mixing bowl, combine all the marinade ingredients thoroughly. Add the prawns [shrimps] and stir well to coat them with the marinade. Set aside in a cool place to marinate for 1 hour.

Remove the prawns [shrimps] from the marinade and pat them dry with kitchen paper towels. Reserve the marinade.

Preheat the grill [broiler] to moderate.

Thread 1 prawn [shrimp] on to a skewer, then a piece of green pepper, a mushroom, sage leaf and a piece of lemon. Repeat the process 3 more times, then fill 3 more skewers in the same way.

Place the skewers on the rack in the grill [broiler] pan and baste them with a little of the reserved marinade.

Place the pan under the heat and grill [broil] the kebabs for 10 minutes, turning them over occasionally and basting with the reserved marinade.

Remove the kebabs from the heat and place them on a warmed serving dish. Pour over the pan juices and serve.

Prawn Savoury is a mouth-watering mixture of prawns, green pepper and sweetcorn, served on toast.

Crab Patties

A special seafood dish from the eastern part of the United States, Crab Patties are a joy to eat.

4-6 SERVINGS

1 lb. crabmeat, shell and cartilage removed

3 oz. [1½ cups] fresh breadcrumbs

1 egg yolk

2 tablespoons mayonnaise

12 spring onions [scallions], finely chopped

1 hard-boiled egg, finely chopped

½ teaspoon chopped fresh marjoram

2 teaspoons lemon juice

¼ teaspoon salt

¼ teaspoon black pepper

⅛ teaspoon cayenne pepper

4 fl. oz. [½ cup] vegetable oil

½ bunch watercress, trimmed and washed

In a medium-sized mixing bowl, combine the crabmeat, breadcrumbs, egg yolk, mayonnaise, spring onions [scallions], hard-boiled egg, marjoram, lemon juice, salt, pepper and cayenne. Mix and knead the mixture with your hands until it comes away from the sides of the bowl. Shape the crab mixture into 2-inch balls, place them on a board and flatten them with the palm of your hands.

In a large frying-pan, heat the vegetable

A spectacular dish for that special occasion, Dublin Bay Prawns served on a bed of rice.

oil over moderately high heat. When the oil is hot, add the patties, a few at a time, and fry them for 3 to 5 minutes on each side or until they are deep golden brown. Using a slotted spoon, transfer the patties to kitchen paper towels to drain.

Place the patties on a warmed serving dish, garnish with the watercress and serve immediately.

Dublin Bay Prawns

A spectacularly attractive main dish for a dinner party, Dublin Bay Prawns taste as good as they look.

4 SERVINGS

SAUCE

4 teaspoons dark brown sugar

½ teaspoon black pepper
¼ teaspoon salt
½ teaspoon ground ginger
2 teaspoons soy sauce
1 teaspoon Worcestershire sauce
8 fl. oz. [1 cup] dry white wine
1 garlic clove, finely chopped
3 teaspoons cornflour [cornstarch]
    dissolved in 3 teaspoons water
RICE
8 oz. [1⅓ cups] long-grain rice,
    washed, soaked in cold water
    for 30 minutes and drained
19 fl. oz. [2⅜ cups] cold water
1 teaspoon salt
PRAWNS
2 lb. Dublin Bay prawns [large
    Gulf shrimps], shelled
¼ teaspoon cayenne pepper
3 tablespoons olive oil
1 large red pepper, white pith
    removed, seeded and cut into
    ½-inch lengths

To make the sauce, in a medium-sized saucepan, combine the sugar, black pepper, salt and ginger. Add the soy sauce, Worcestershire sauce and wine and mix thoroughly. Add the garlic.

Place the pan over high heat and bring the sauce to the boil. Reduce the heat to low, cover the pan and simmer for 20 minutes.

Remove the pan from the heat and stir in the cornflour [cornstarch]. Return the pan to high heat and bring the mixture to the boil. Reduce the heat to low and simmer for 5 minutes, or until the sauce thickens. Remove the pan from the heat.

Place the rice, water and salt in a large saucepan. Bring to the boil over high heat. Cover the pan, reduce the heat to very low and simmer for 15 minutes. If all the liquid is not absorbed at the end of this time, continue to cook, uncovered, until the rice is dry. Transfer the rice to a warmed serving dish and keep warm.

Meanwhile, sprinkle the prawns with the cayenne. In a large frying-pan, heat the oil over moderate heat. Add the prawns and red pepper to the pan and cook, turning frequently, for 10 minutes.

While the prawns are cooking, reheat the sauce, stirring, over low heat.

Arrange the prawns on top of the rice, pour the hot sauce over them and serve.

Oranges Stuffed with Prawns or Shrimps and Rice

A tangy first course, Oranges Stuffed with Prawns or Shrimps and Rice makes an attractive and tasty dish. Serve on a bed of chopped lettuce.

6 SERVINGS
6 medium-sized oranges, halved
2½ oz. [1 cup] cooked long-grain rice
6 oz. prawns or shrimps, shelled
2 oz. [⅓ cup] raisins
2 oz. [½ cup] slivered almonds
DRESSING
3 tablespoons olive oil
1 tablespoon red wine vinegar
½ teaspoon salt
¼ teaspoon black pepper
½ teaspoon dried thyme

First, prepare the dressing. In a small mixing bowl, beat the oil, vinegar, salt, pepper and thyme together with a fork until they are well combined. Set aside.

Using a serrated-edged knife, carefully cut out the flesh from the oranges, until only the shell is left. Set the shells aside.

Place the orange flesh on a chopping board and cut it into small cubes, discarding any membrane. Transfer the cubes to a medium-sized mixing bowl. Add the rice, prawns or shrimps, raisins and almonds. Spoon over the prepared dressing and mix until all the ingredients are well coated.

Place the bowl in the refrigerator to chill for 30 minutes.

Remove the bowl from the refrigerator. Spoon the orange and rice mixture into the reserved orange shells and serve.

Oysters Kilpatrick - simple to make, beautiful to eat.

Oysters Kilpatrick

Serve this simple but delicious dish with a glass of iced-cold lager and slices of brown bread and butter.

3 SERVINGS
2 oz. [¼ cup] butter, softened
32 fresh oysters, with one shell
    removed
2 teaspoons Worcestershire sauce
12 lean bacon slices, grilled [broiled]
    until crisp and crumbled
2 tablespoons chopped parsley

Preheat the grill [broiler] to moderate.

Using a flat-bladed knife, carefully spread a thin layer of butter over each oyster. Season the oysters with the Worcestershire sauce and sprinkle over the crumbled bacon.

Place the oysters, a few at a time, under the grill [broiler] and grill [broil] for 2 minutes. Remove the oysters from the grill [broiler] and keep warm while you grill [broil] the remaining oysters in the same way.

Sprinkle over the parsley and serve immediately.

Stuffed Squid makes a festive centre-piece to any family meal.

Scallops Sautéed with Garlic and Basil

 ① ① ① ⊠

This simple recipe for scallops is an exquisite first course for a special dinner.

4 SERVINGS

juice of ½ lemon
¼ teaspoon salt
¼ teaspoon white pepper
1½ lb. scallops, cut into ½-inch pieces
2½ oz. [⅝ cup] flour
6 tablespoons vegetable oil
3 shallots, finely chopped
3 garlic cloves, crushed
¼ teaspoon dried basil
1 oz. [2 tablespoons] butter
1 tablespoon chopped parsley

Sprinkle the lemon juice, salt and pepper over the scallops. Put the scallops in a strainer and sprinkle the flour over them.

In a frying-pan heat half the oil over moderate heat. The oil should cover the pan in a thin film, so if necessary add the rest.

Add the scallops and toss lightly. Cook the scallops for 5 minutes or until they are lightly browned. Add the shallots, garlic and basil to the pan and cook for 2 minutes. Remove the pan from the heat, stir in the butter and parsley and transfer the scallops to individual warmed serving dishes. Serve immediately.

Stuffed Squid

 ① ①

Squid stuffed with a cheese, garlic and parsley mixture and cooked in a wine and tomato sauce is an unusual main dish for a family dinner.

3 SERVINGS

6 medium-sized squid, cleaned and skinned with the tender parts of the tentacles reserved
3 tablespoons fresh breadcrumbs
2 tablespoons finely chopped parsley
6 tablespoons grated Parmesan cheese
2 garlic cloves, finely chopped plus 4 whole garlic cloves
1 egg, lightly beaten
2 fl. oz. [¼ cup] olive oil
⅛ teaspoon cayenne pepper
½ teaspoon salt
¼ teaspoon black pepper

14 oz. canned peeled Italian plum tomatoes
½ teaspoon dried rosemary
2 fl. oz. [¼ cup] dry white wine

Chop the tentacles finely and place them in a mixing bowl. Add the breadcrumbs, parsley, cheese, 1 chopped garlic clove, the egg, 1 tablespoon of olive oil, cayenne, ¼ teaspoon of salt and ⅛ teaspoon of pepper to the bowl. Mix well.

Spoon the mixture into the squid.

With a thick needle and thread, sew up the openings of each squid.

In a large, deep frying-pan, heat the remaining oil over moderate heat. Add the whole garlic cloves to the pan and cook them for 5 minutes, stirring. Remove and discard the garlic cloves.

Add the squid to the pan and brown them on all sides, turning carefully. Add the tomatoes with the can juice, rosemary, the remaining chopped garlic, the wine, and the rest of the salt and pepper.

Reduce the heat to low, cover the pan and simmer gently for 20 to 30 minutes.

Remove the squid from the pan and place them on a plate. Remove and discard the thread. Slice the squid and arrange the slices in a warmed serving dish. Pour over the sauce and serve.

Fish and seafood for entertaining

It's not often that people think of entertaining around a fish main course — probably partly a holdover from the formal days of eating when there was a 'fish' course to precede the main or meat offering, but also perhaps partly due to plain ignorance of just how superb, and festive, fish can be. For whatever the reason, prospective guests are the ultimate losers, for fish can provide some of the most nourishing and varied dishes around today.

Fish dishes can be as expensive or as cheap as you care to make them, from the dizzy gourmet heights of Salmon with Dill Mayonnaise (page 42), through elegant Crabmeat and Avocado Mousse (page 54), to delicate, inexpensive Truro Skate with Egg and Lemon Sauce (page 49). And they span the unusual and familiar, too — like exotic Stir-fried Abalone and Chinese Cabbage (pictured below, recipe on page 62), or classic Trout with Almonds (page 46).

For those occasions when there's someone coming to dinner you simply CAN'T put off and coffers are low, there's a whole, colourful **For Budget Occasions** section containing easy-to-make fish and seafood dinners guaranteed to have them coming back for more!

All of them, from the grandest to the more modest, are specially chosen for their ease of preparation and relatively short cooking times — thus giving you time to change your dress, powder your nose, and generally meet and greet your guests the way you want to, feeling relaxed.

Bass with White Butter Sauce

Decorative and easy to prepare, Bass with White Butter Sauce is an ideal main course for a lunch or dinner party, served with new potatoes and courgettes [zucchini] sautéed in butter. A white Burgundy is a good accompaniment.

6 SERVINGS

5 pints [6¼ pints] court bouillon or fish stock
1 x 3 lb. sea bass, cleaned, with the head and tail left on
6 parsley sprigs
SAUCE
2 fl. oz. [¼ cup] white wine vinegar
2 fl. oz. [¼ cup] dry white wine
3 shallots, finely chopped
½ teaspoon salt
¼ teaspoon white pepper
8 oz. [1 cup] unsalted butter, cut into small pieces and chilled

Pour the court bouillon or stock into a large fish kettle and bring it to the boil over high heat.

Meanwhile, wash the fish thoroughly, inside and out, under cold running water. Pat dry with kitchen paper towels and carefully wrap it in a double piece of cheesecloth.

Reduce the heat to low. Place the fish on the rack of the kettle, and lower the rack into the kettle. (The liquid should cover the fish by 2 inches.)

Cover the kettle and simmer the fish very gently for 15 minutes. Remove the kettle from the heat and set aside for 15 minutes.

Lift the fish out of the kettle and transfer it to a large chopping board. Carefully remove and discard the cheese-cloth. Carefully remove the skin from the fish with a sharp knife. Arrange the fish on a large serving plate and garnish with the parsley sprigs. Keep warm.

To make the sauce, put the vinegar, wine, shallots, salt and pepper into a medium-sized saucepan. Set the pan over moderate heat and bring the liquid to the boil. Cook, stirring occasionally, until the liquid is reduced to about 1 tablespoon.

Remove the pan from the heat and, with a wire whisk, stir in 4 small pieces of the chilled butter, beating constantly until it is completely absorbed.

Return the pan to very low heat and add the rest of the chilled butter, a small piece at a time, whisking constantly and making sure all the butter is absorbed before adding the next piece. Remove the pan from the heat and pour the sauce into a warmed sauceboat.

Serve the fish at once, accompanied by the sauce.

Easy to prepare, delicious to eat - Bass with White Butter Sauce makes an elegant centrepiece for a special lunch or dinner.

Bream [Porgy] with Fresh Fennel in White Wine

A delicate, aromatic blend of fresh herbs and wine, Bream [Porgy] with Fresh Fennel in White Wine is a simple, yet sophisticated Mediterranean dish. It may be served with boiled new potatoes and petits pois, and accompanied by a well-chilled white Rhine wine, such as Rüdesheimer.

4 SERVINGS

1 x 2 lb. bream [porgy], cleaned and gutted
2 sprigs fresh fennel leaves
2 sprigs fresh thyme
1 oz. [2 tablespoons] butter
½ teaspoon salt
½ teaspoon freshly ground black pepper
5 fl. oz. [⅝ cup] dry white wine
1 tablespoon olive oil
1 fresh fennel, trimmed and sliced
2 tomatoes, sliced
1 lemon, thinly sliced

Preheat the oven to moderate 350°F (Gas Mark 4, 180°C).

With a small, sharp knife, make 2 deep incisions along the back of the fish. Insert the fennel sprigs in the incisions.

Place the thyme and the butter inside the fish. Sprinkle the fish with the salt and pepper.

Place the fish on a rack in a large roasting tin.

Pour the wine and olive oil over the fish, and arrange the fennel, tomatoes and lemon slices on top.

Place the fish in the oven and bake it for about 30 minutes, or until the fish flakes easily when tested with a fork. Baste the fish occasionally with the cooking liquid during cooking.

Carefully transfer the fish to a large shallow serving dish and serve immediately.

Brill with Courgettes [Zucchini]

This delicious dish is surprisingly easy to cook and makes a perfect main course for a dinner party.

4 SERVINGS

3 oz. [⅜ cup] butter
2 lb. brill fillets
1 teaspoon lemon juice

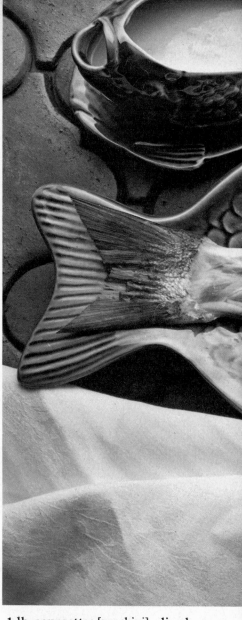

1 lb. courgettes [zucchini], sliced
¾ teaspoon salt
¼ teaspoon black pepper
½ teaspoon dried basil
4 tablespoons flour
10 fl. oz. [1¼ cups] milk
1 tablespoon grated cheese

Preheat the oven to moderate 350°F (Gas Mark 4, 180°C).

Grease a shallow baking dish with 1 tablespoon butter. Put the fillets in the baking dish and pour in the lemon juice and just enough water to cover. Poach the fillets in the oven for 15 to 20 minutes, or until the fish flakes easily.

Transfer the fish to a flameproof serving dish and keep warm. Strain the liquid from the baking dish and reserve.

Meanwhile, melt 2 tablespoons of the butter in a saucepan over moderate heat. Add the courgette [zucchini] slices to it. Stir, cover and simmer for about 8 minutes, or until they are just tender. Stir in ½ teaspoon salt, pepper and basil. Place to one side and keep hot.

Preheat the grill [broiler] to moderate.

In another saucepan, melt the remaining butter over moderate heat. Remove the saucepan from the heat and stir in the flour with a wooden spoon. Add the milk and the liquid from the fish, stirring constantly until the mixture is smooth. Replace the pan on the heat and bring the sauce to the boil. Stirring constantly, boil the sauce for 5 minutes. Stir in the remaining salt. Taste the sauce for seasoning and add more salt if necessary.

Pour the sauce over the fish. Sprinkle on the cheese and brown under the grill [broiler]. Surround with the drained courgette [zucchini] slices and serve immediately.

Carp Jewish-Style

☆ ☆   ① ⃝   ⊠ ⊠ ⊠

Cold carp set in jellied stock is a fine flavoured light dish for the summer. Serve it with a variety of salads and a well chilled Hungarian Riesling. This dish may also be served hot.

6 SERVINGS

3 fish heads
2 pints [5 cups] cold water
1 medium-sized onion, thinly sliced
1 bay leaf
1 teaspoon freshly ground black pepper
1 teaspoon salt
1 clove
2 medium-sized carrots, scraped and diced
1 medium-sized kohlrabi, peeled and diced
2 celery stalks, trimmed and sliced
1 tablespoon lemon juice
1 tablespoon white wine vinegar
1 tablespoon sugar
3 lb. carp, cut into steaks

Put the fish heads and the water in a large saucepan. Add the onion, bay leaf, pepper, salt and clove. Place the pan over high heat and bring the water to the boil. Reduce the heat to moderately low. Cover the pan and simmer the mixture for 30

minutes.

Remove the pan from the heat and strain the stock into a bowl. Discard the fish heads and seasonings. Return the stock to the pan. Add the carrots, kohlrabi and celery and return the pan to moderate heat. Bring to the boil. Cover the pan, reduce the heat to low and simmer for 20 to 30 minutes or until the vegetables are tender.

Stir in the lemon juice, vinegar and sugar. Place the fish steaks on top of the vegetables, cover the pan and simmer for 15 to 20 minutes or until the fish flakes easily when tested with a fork.

Remove the pan from the heat. With a slotted spoon, carefully transfer the fish steaks to a large serving dish. Pour the liquid and the vegetables over the fish and set aside to cool.

Cover the dish and place it in the refrigerator to chill for 1 hour, basting occasionally so that a glaze forms on the fish.

When the cooking liquid has set to a firm jelly, remove the dish from the refrigerator and serve immediately.

Baked Halibut Fillets

Baked Halibut Fillets makes a superb lunch or dinner party dish, served with croquette potatoes and sautéed mushrooms. Accompany with a well-chilled white Moselle wine.

4 SERVINGS

4 halibut fillets
½ teaspoon salt
¼ teaspoon black pepper
5 fl. oz. double cream [⅝ cup heavy cream]
8 fl. oz. [1 cup] dry white wine
1 bay leaf
1 tablespoon chopped fresh chives
½ teaspoon dried chervil
1 tablespoon lemon juice
1 tablespoon cornflour [cornstarch] dissolved in 2 tablespoons white wine
2 oz. [½ cup] Parmesan cheese, grated

Preheat the oven to fairly hot 375°F (Gas Mark 5, 190°C).

Rub the fish fillets all over with the salt and pepper and arrange them in a large ovenproof dish. Set the dish aside.

In a medium-sized mixing bowl, combine the cream, wine, bay leaf, chives,

Halibut Steaks with Green Peppercorns makes a luxurious dish for special entertaining.

chervil, lemon juice and the cornflour [cornstarch] mixture.

Pour the sauce over the fish in the baking dish. Sprinkle on the grated cheese.

Place the dish in the centre of the oven and bake for 25 to 30 minutes, or until the cheese has melted and the fish flakes easily when tested with a fork.

Remove the dish from the oven. Remove and discard the bay leaf. Serve immediately, straight from the dish.

Halibut Steaks with Green Peppercorns

This luxurious mixture of halibut, green peppercorns, tomatoes, cream and brandy is an unusual dinner party dish. Serve with croquette potatoes, steamed broccoli and, to drink, some well chilled white wine such as Pouilly Fumé.

4 SERVINGS

4 halibut steaks
1 teaspoon salt

1 tablespoon lemon juice
1 large garlic clove, crushed
1½ oz. [3 tablespoons] butter
4 medium-sized tomatoes, blanched, peeled, seeded and finely chopped
4 tablespoons canned green peppercorns, drained
1 tablespoon French mustard
2 fl. oz. [¼ cup] sour cream
4 fl. oz. double cream [½ cup heavy cream]
2 tablespoons brandy

Rub the fish steaks all over with the salt, lemon juice and garlic and set them aside on a plate.

In a frying-pan large enough to hold all the fish steaks in one layer, melt the butter over moderate heat. When the foam subsides, add the tomatoes, peppercorns and mustard and cook the mixture, stirring frequently, for 6 to 8 minutes or until it is thick.

Stir in the sour cream and place the fish in the pan. Spoon over the tomato mixture and reduce the heat to moderately low. Cook the fish for 8 to 10 minutes on each side or until the flesh flakes easily when tested with a fork.

Using a slotted spoon, remove the fish from the pan and transfer it to a warmed serving dish. Keep hot while you finish the sauce.

Stir the double [heavy] cream and brandy into the sauce and cook, stirring constantly, for 5 minutes.

Remove the pan from the heat, pour the sauce over the fish and serve.

Halibut Steaks with Tomatoes and Cream

 ① ① ① ☒

This simple dish makes an excellent lunch or dinner. Serve with boiled rice or croquette potatoes.

4 SERVINGS

1 oz. [2 tablespoons] butter
1 large onion, thinly sliced and pushed out into rings
14 oz. canned peeled tomatoes, roughly chopped
1 teaspoon dried marjoram
½ teaspoon salt
¼ teaspoon black pepper
4 halibut steaks
8 oz. small button mushrooms, wiped clean and halved
5 fl. oz. double cream [⅝ cup heavy cream]

In a flameproof casserole, melt the butter over moderate heat. When the foam subsides, add the onion and cook, stirring occasionally, for 5 to 7 minutes, or until it is soft and translucent but not brown.

Stir in the tomatoes and the can juice, marjoram, salt and pepper. Add the fish steaks. Bring the liquid to the boil, stirring occasionally. Reduce the heat to low, cover and simmer for 8 minutes on each side.

Stir the mushrooms and cream into the casserole and cook, stirring occasionally, for a further 2 minutes, or until the sauce is hot but not boiling and the fish flakes easily when tested with a fork.

Remove the casserole from the heat and turn the mixture out into a warmed serving dish. Serve immediately.

Halibut Stuffed with Shrimps and Crabmeat

 ① ① ① ☒ ☒

Serve this marvellous dinner party dish with fried rice and a tomato salad and accompany with a well-chilled white Moselle wine.

6 SERVINGS

4 oz. canned crabmeat
2 oz. [¼ cup] plus 1 teaspoon butter
8 oz. shrimps, shelled
2 tablespoons flour
8 fl. oz. [1 cup] fish stock
2 fl. oz. double cream [¼ cup heavy cream]
2 fl. oz. [¼ cup] dry white wine
4 oz. mushrooms, chopped
1 small green pepper, white pith

An unusual and delicate dish - that's Halibut Stuffed with Shrimps and Crabmeat.

removed, seeded and chopped
2 oz. [1 cup] cooked rice
½ teaspoon salt
¼ teaspoon black pepper
1 x 3 lb. tail end of halibut, centre bone removed
2 oz. [¼ cup] butter, melted
parsley sprigs
lemon wedges

Remove any shell and cartilage from the crabmeat and set aside.

Preheat the oven to moderate 350°F (Gas Mark 4, 180°C). Lightly grease a large shallow baking dish with the teaspoon of butter. Set aside.

In a large frying-pan, melt the remaining butter over moderate heat. When the foam subsides, reduce the heat to low and add the crabmeat and shrimps to the pan, stirring with a wooden spoon until they are well coated in butter. Stir in the flour.

Pour in the stock, cream and wine, stirring constantly until they are blended. Heat gently until the liquid is hot but not boiling. Stir in the mushrooms, green pepper, rice, salt and pepper. Remove the pan from the heat and spoon the mixture into the pocket of the halibut.

Spread the excess mixture over the bottom of the baking dish. Arrange the stuffed fish on top and pour over the melted butter. Cover and place in the oven. Bake the fish for 50 minutes, or until it is tender but still firm.

Remove the dish from the oven and serve the fish at once, garnished with the parsley and lemon.

Mullets with Bacon and Peas

An unusual combination of fish with the savoury flavour of bacon, Mullets with Bacon and Peas make an attractive and colourful dish. Serve with creamed potatoes and grilled [broiled] tomatoes.

6 SERVINGS

6 streaky bacon slices, finely chopped
1 medium-sized onion, finely chopped
3 oz. [¾ cup] seasoned flour, made with 3 oz. [¾ cup] flour, ½ teaspoon salt, ¼ teaspoon black pepper and ¼ teaspoon paprika
6 medium-sized red mullets, cleaned and with the eyes removed
4 oz. [½ cup] butter
1 tablespoon soft brown sugar
1 lb. fresh peas, weighed after shelling
1 teaspoon salt
½ teaspoon black pepper
½ teaspoon finely chopped fresh thyme or ¼ teaspoon dried thyme
10 fl. oz. [1¼ cups] chicken stock
4 fl. oz. [½ cup] dry white wine
1 tablespoon cornflour [cornstarch] dissolved in 2 tablespoons water

In a medium-sized frying-pan, fry the bacon over moderately high heat, stirring occasionally, for 5 to 8 minutes or until it is crisp and brown and has rendered most of its fat. With a slotted spoon, transfer the bacon from the pan to a plate and keep warm.

Reduce the heat to moderate and add the onion to the frying-pan. Fry, stirring occasionally, for 5 to 7 minutes, or until it is soft and translucent but not brown. Remove the pan from the heat and, with a slotted spoon, transfer the onion to the plate with the bacon.

Place the seasoned flour in a large shallow dish. Dip the fish in the flour mixture, shaking off any excess. Set them aside.

Add half of the butter to the fat in the frying-pan and return it to moderate heat. When the foam subsides, add the fish, three at a time, and fry them for 5 minutes on each side, or until the flesh flakes easily when tested with a fork. Transfer the fish to a warmed serving dish and keep warm while you fry the remaining fish in the same way, using the remaining butter. Keep the fish warm while you prepare the sauce.

Reduce the heat to low and add the onion, bacon and brown sugar to the pan. Cook, stirring constantly with a wooden spoon, for 3 minutes, or until the sugar has completely dissolved.

Add the peas, salt, black pepper, thyme, chicken stock and white wine. Increase the heat to high and bring the mixture to the boil, stirring occasionally.

Reduce the heat to moderately low and simmer for 10 to 12 minutes, or until the peas are tender. Remove the pan from the heat.

Stir in the dissolved cornflour [cornstarch] and return the pan to the heat. Cook the sauce, stirring constantly, for 2 to 3 minutes or until it thickens and is smooth.

Remove the pan from the heat and spoon the sauce over the fish. Serve immediately.

Mullet Baked in Rock Salt

A delectable dish with a special fragrant flavour, Mullet Baked in Rock Salt may be served with green beans and an apple and onion salad for an informal lunch or dinner party.

4 SERVINGS

12 oz. [2 cups] rock salt
1 x 4 lb. grey mullet, cleaned but with the head left on
1 teaspoon chopped fresh chives or ½ teaspoon dried chives
1 teaspoon chopped fresh tarragon or ½ teaspoon dried tarragon
1 rosemary sprig
juice of 1 lemon

Preheat the oven to warm 325°F (Gas Mark 3, 170°C).

Cover the bottom of a large, deep ovenproof dish with approximately one-third of the rock salt. Place the fish on top of the salt. Sprinkle over the chives and tarragon and place the rosemary sprig on top. Sprinkle over the lemon juice. Pour in the remaining rock salt to surround and cover the fish completely. With the back of a wooden spoon carefully pat down the salt.

Place the dish in the centre of the oven and bake the fish for 50 minutes to 1 hour.

Remove the dish from the oven. Using a weight, such as a rolling pin or pestle, break the hardened crust of the salt. With a sharp knife, prise the salt off and discard it.

Serve the fish at once, straight from the dish.

Mullets Baked with Shrimps

A simple, tasty dish originating from West Africa, Red Mullets Baked with Shrimps

may be served with rice or hot crusty bread. Accompany with a light well-chilled Moselle wine, such as Bernkasteler or Moselblumchen for a colourful lunch or supper.

4 SERVINGS

3 fl. oz. [⅜ cup] lemon juice
2 fl. oz. [¼ cup] water
1 tablespoon Worcestershire sauce
3 fl. oz. [⅜ cup] tomato ketchup
1 teaspoon finely chopped fresh rosemary or ½ teaspoon dried rosemary
6 peppercorns
4 red mullets, cleaned and with the eyes removed
1 oz. [2 tablespoons] butter
8 oz. shrimps, shelled and deveined
3 fl. oz. [⅜ cup] olive oil or peanut oil
1 lemon, thinly sliced
1 bunch watercress, washed and shaken dry

In a large mixing bowl, combine the lemon juice, water, Worcestershire sauce, tomato ketchup, rosemary and peppercorns and beat well with a fork until the ingredients are thoroughly combined. Place the fish in the mixture. Cover the bowl and set aside to marinate for at least 30 minutes, at room temperature, basting the fish with the marinade from time to time.

Preheat the oven to moderate 350°F (Gas Mark 4, 180°C).

With 1 tablespoon of the butter, grease an ovenproof dish large enough to take all of the mullets in one layer. Carefully remove the mullets from the marinade. Discard the marinade.

Arrange the fish in the dish, cut the remaining butter into small pieces and dot them over the fish. Scatter the shrimps over the fish, then pour over the oil.

Place the dish in the centre of the oven and bake the fish, basting occasionally with the oil, for 20 to 30 minutes or until the flesh flakes easily when tested with a fork.

Remove the dish from the oven. Transfer the fish to a warmed serving dish and pour over the cooking juices. Garnish the fish with the lemon slices and the watercress.

Serve immediately.

Colourful Mullets Baked with Shrimps is an adaptation of a West African dish. Garnished (as here) with lemon and watercress and served on a bed of rice, it makes an exotic dish for an informal dinner.

Pike Stuffed with Cucumber and Rice

☆ ☆ ① ① ✕ ✕

This delightful Scandinavian dish is ideal to serve hot at a dinner party. It can also be eaten cold.

6-8 SERVINGS

1 x 3½ lb. pike, cleaned and gutted, with the head and tail left on and the backbone removed
1 teaspoon salt
½ teaspoon black pepper
4 oz. [½ cup] butter
2 onions, chopped
4 spring onions [scallions], trimmed and finely chopped
3 oz. [½ cup] long-grain rice, washed, soaked in cold water for 30 minutes and drained
1 cucumber, peeled and chopped
1 tablespoon chopped fresh chives
1 teaspoon grated lemon rind
1 tablespoon finely chopped fresh coriander leaves
8 fl. oz. [1 cup] dry white wine

Sprinkle the fish, inside and out, with half of the salt and pepper. Set aside.

Preheat the oven to moderate 350°F (Gas Mark 4, 180°C).

In a large frying-pan, melt half of the butter over moderate heat. When the foam subsides, add the onions and spring onions [scallions] and fry, stirring frequently, for 5 to 7 minutes or until the onions are soft and translucent but not brown. Add the rice, cucumber, chives, lemon rind, coriander leaves and remaining salt and pepper and fry, stirring constantly, for a further 5 minutes.

Remove the frying-pan from the heat and set aside to cool.

Stuff the mixture into the cavity of the fish. Sew up the cavity with a trussing needle and string.

Place the fish in a large baking tin. Cut the remaining butter into small pieces and dot them over the fish. Pour over the wine and place the tin in the centre of the oven. Bake the fish, basting occasionally, for 35 to 45 minutes or until the flesh flakes easily when tested with a fork.

Remove the tin from the oven. Transfer the fish to a warmed serving dish. Pour over the cooking juices and serve at once.

Fluffy and rich and easy to make - that's Plaice [Flounder] Anatole!

Plaice [Flounder] **Anatole**

A delicious soufflé-like dish, Plaice [Flounder] Anatole is quick and easy to make.

4-6 SERVINGS

2 oz. [¼ cup] plus 1 teaspoon butter
2 lb. plaice [flounder] fillets
1 large green pepper, white pith removed, seeded and sliced
1 pint [2½ cups] mayonnaise
8 oz. [2 cups] Cheddar cheese, grated
½ teaspoon salt
¼ teaspoon white pepper
2 fl. oz. double cream [¼ cup heavy cream]
4 egg whites, stiffly beaten

Preheat the oven to moderate 350°F (Gas Mark 4, 180°C). With the teaspoon of butter, grease a large ovenproof dish.

In a frying-pan, melt the remaining butter over moderate heat. When the foam subsides, add the plaice [flounder] fillets, a few at a time, and fry for 2 minutes on each side. Remove the pan from the heat and remove the skin from the fish fillets. Transfer the fillets to the prepared dish. Arrange the green pepper slices over the fish and set aside.

Place the mayonnaise in a mixing bowl. Stir in the cheese, salt and pepper and then the cream. With a metal spoon, carefully fold in the beaten egg whites until the mixture is thoroughly combined.

Pour the mixture over the fish. Place the dish in the oven and bake for 20 minutes or until the top has turned golden brown.

Remove from the oven and serve.

Red Snapper with Almond and Walnut Sauce

A delicately flavoured dish to tempt everyone, Red Snapper with Almond and Walnut Sauce is surprisingly easy to make.

6 SERVINGS

3 lb. red snapper fillets
2 oz. [½ cup] seasoned flour, made with 2 oz. [½ cup] flour, 1 teaspoon salt and ½ teaspoon white pepper
2 oz. [¼ cup] butter
SAUCE
1½ oz. [3 tablespoons] butter
1½ oz. [6 tablespoons] flour
8 fl. oz. single cream [1 cup light cream]
10 fl. oz. [1¼ cups] dry white wine
1 teaspoon dried marjoram
½ teaspoon salt
½ teaspoon black pepper
2 oz. [½ cup] slivered almonds
2 oz. [½ cup] walnuts, chopped
4 oz. [1 cup] Gruyère cheese, grated

Preheat the oven to moderate 350°F (Gas

Delicately flavoured Red Snapper with Almond and Walnut Sauce.

Mark 4, 180°C).

Dip the fish fillets into the seasoned flour to coat them thoroughly.

In a large frying-pan, melt the butter over moderate heat. When the foam subsides, fry the fillets, a few at a time, for 5 minutes on each side or until they are golden brown all over, adding more butter if necessary. Remove the pan from the heat. With a slotted spoon, remove the fillets from the pan and transfer them to a large, shallow ovenproof dish.

In a medium-sized saucepan, melt the butter over moderate heat. With a wooden spoon, stir in the flour. Remove the pan from the heat and gradually add the cream, stirring constantly and being careful to avoid lumps.

Stir in the wine, marjoram, salt, pepper, almonds and walnuts. Return the pan to the heat and bring the sauce to the boil, stirring constantly. Reduce the heat to low and simmer the sauce for 5 minutes, stirring frequently.

Remove the pan from the heat and pour the sauce over the fish.

Sprinkle the cheese over the sauce and place the dish in the centre of the oven. Bake the fish for 15 to 20 minutes or until the cheese has melted and is golden brown. Serve immediately.

Salmon

Sumptuous Salmon with Dill Mayonnaise is the ideal party dish.

While the salmon is cooling, make the sauce. Pour the mayonnaise and cream into a mixing bowl and stir in the reserved cooking liquid, the lemon juice, pepper, salt, cayenne and mustard. Stir until the sauce is smooth and evenly coloured. Fold in the dill and shrimps and set aside.

Place the lettuce, cress, radishes, lemon juice and vinegar in a mixing bowl and toss well with two large spoons.

Line the bottom of a large serving platter with the lettuce mixture. Place the salmon in the centre of the dish and spoon over the sauce to cover the salmon completely.

Arrange the tomatoes, hard-boiled eggs and spring onions [scallions] decoratively around the salmon and serve immediately.

Salmon Roll

Salmon Roll is an ideal dish to eke out fresh salmon flesh taken from the head and tail. Serve as a light luncheon dish with sour cream.

3-4 SERVINGS

2 teaspoons butter
10 oz. cooked fresh salmon, skinned
4 eggs, separated
1 oz. [2 tablespoons] butter, melted
3 tablespoons flour
½ teaspoon salt
½ teaspoon black pepper
2 teaspoons chopped fresh chives
1 teaspoon chopped fresh fennel
½ teaspoon chopped fresh marjoram
2 teaspoons white wine vinegar
2 tablespoons double [heavy] cream

With 1 teaspoon of the butter, grease a 7- x 10-inch baking tin. Line the tin with greaseproof or waxed paper, allowing the paper to stand 1-inch above the sides of the tin. Grease the paper with the remaining butter. Preheat the oven to moderate 350°F (Gas Mark 4, 180°C).

Purée the salmon in a blender or food mill. Set aside.

Place the egg yolks in a mixing bowl and, using a wooden spoon, beat them until they are thick and pale. Gradually beat in the melted butter. Stir in the flour, a tablespoon at a time, and beat until the ingredients are combined.

Stir in the salmon, salt, pepper, chives, fennel, marjoram, vinegar and cream and beat until the mixture is smooth.

In another large mixing bowl, beat the egg whites with a wire whisk or rotary

Salmon with Dill Mayonnaise

This splendid cold dish may be served as a complete summer dinner party meal with crusty French bread and butter and parsley potatoes. A well-chilled Pouilly Fumé would be the ideal accompaniment.

6 SERVINGS

1 x 5 lb. salmon, cleaned
2 lemons, thinly sliced
6 black peppercorns
½ teaspoon dried dill
1½ teaspoons salt
2 small shallots, sliced
2 small bay leaves
10 fl. oz. [1¼ cups] dry white wine
SAUCE
10 fl. oz. [1¼ cups] mayonnaise
2 fl. oz. double cream [¼ cup heavy cream]
2 teaspoons lemon juice
¼ teaspoon black pepper
¼ teaspoon salt
¼ teaspoon cayenne pepper
½ teaspoon French mustard
1 tablespoon chopped fresh dill
6 oz. small peeled frozen shrimps, thawed and drained
GARNISH
1 medium-sized round [Boston] lettuce, outer leaves removed, washed and shredded
1 medium-sized bunch mustard and cress, washed and shaken dry
10 small radishes, very thinly sliced
1 teaspoon lemon juice
1 teaspoon tarragon vinegar
6 medium-sized tomatoes, sliced
6 hard-boiled eggs, sliced
6 spring onions [scallions], trimmed

Wash the salmon in cold water and dry with kitchen paper towels.

Line the bottom of a fish kettle or flameproof casserole with the lemon slices. Sprinkle over the peppercorns, dill, salt, shallot slices and bay leaves. Place the salmon in the kettle or casserole and pour over the wine.

Place the kettle or casserole over high heat and bring the wine to the boil. Reduce the heat to low, cover and simmer the salmon for 40 to 50 minutes or until the flesh flakes easily.

Remove the kettle or casserole from the heat. Using two large spoons, remove the salmon from the kettle or casserole and place it on a flat working surface. Strain the cooking liquid and reserve 3 tablespoons, discarding the rest.

Carefully skin the salmon, being careful not to break up the flesh.

Set the salmon aside to cool completely.

42

beater until they form stiff peaks.

With a large metal spoon, carefully fold the egg whites into the salmon mixture until they are thoroughly combined.

Pour the salmon mixture into the tin and smooth the top with a table knife. Place the tin in the oven and bake the mixture for 15 minutes or until it is just firm to the touch and pale golden brown.

Remove the tin from the oven. Turn the mixture out on to a large piece of greaseproof or waxed paper. Remove the paper from the mixture. With the help of the greaseproof or waxed paper, roll up the mixture Swiss [jelly] roll style. Transfer to a warmed serving dish and serve.

Salmon Steaks Florentine

 ① ① ① ⊠

This superb dish tastes as magnificent as it looks — and it's easy to prepare too!

4 SERVINGS

4 salmon steaks, cut 1-inch thick
2 oz. [¼ cup] unsalted butter, melted
3 lb. spinach, cooked, drained and kept hot
2 fl. oz. double cream [¼ cup heavy cream]
¼ teaspoon salt
¼ teaspoon black pepper
SAUCE
6 oz. [¾ cup] butter, melted
juice of ½ lemon
¼ teaspoon salt
¼ teaspoon white pepper
⅛ teaspoon cayenne pepper

Preheat the grill [broiler] to moderate. Line the pan with aluminium foil.

Place the salmon steaks on the rack and coat them with a little of the melted butter. Place the pan under the grill [broiler] and grill [broil] the steaks for 8 to 10 minutes on each side, basting with the remaining melted butter, or until they are lightly browned and the flesh flakes easily.

Meanwhile, in a large mixing bowl, combine the spinach, cream, salt and pepper, stirring gently until they are blended. Arrange the mixture over the bottom of a warmed, large serving dish.

In a jug, combine all the sauce ingredients, beating until they are well blended.

Remove the steaks from the heat and arrange them on top of the spinach mixture. Pour over the butter sauce and serve at once.

Elegant Smoked Salmon Canapés.

Smoked Salmon Canapés

 ① ① ① ⊠

Luxurious and easy-to-prepare cocktail snacks, Smoked Salmon Canapés may be served as an appetizer before dinner.

24 CANAPES

6 large slices brown bread, crusts removed
4 oz. cream cheese
4 oz. smoked salmon, sliced and cut into 24 pieces
2 tablespoons lemon juice
1 small onion, sliced and pushed out into rings
2 oz. black caviar or lumpfish roe
6 parsley sprigs
1 lemon, cut into wedges

Place the bread slices on a wooden board. Using a sharp knife, cut each slice into 4 diamond shapes. Discard the bread trimmings.

Spread each shape with cream cheese. Cover each one with a piece of smoked salmon. Sprinkle a little lemon juice over the salmon and top with an onion ring. Place a little caviar or lumpfish roe in the centre of each onion ring.

Place the canapés on a decorative serving dish. Garnish with the parsley and lemon wedges and serve at once.

Sole Normande

SOLE FILLETS WITH MUSSELS AND
SHRIMPS

*A classic way to cook sole, Sole Normande
is garnished with shellfish and mushrooms
and has a rich creamy sauce poured over
the top.*

4 SERVINGS

8 sole fillets, skinned
1 pint mussels, scrubbed, steamed
  and cooking liquid reserved, or
  4 oz. canned mussels, can juice
  reserved
1 onion, thinly sliced and pushed
  out into rings
  bouquet garni, consisting of 4
  parsley sprigs, 1 thyme spray and
  1 bay leaf tied together
10 fl. oz. [1¼ cups] dry white wine
1 oz. [2 tablespoons] butter
4 shallots, halved
8 oz. button mushrooms, wiped
  clean and stalks removed
1 tablespoon lemon juice
½ teaspoon salt
¼ teaspoon black pepper
4 oz. frozen shrimps, thawed

SAUCE
1 tablespoon butter
2 tablespoons flour
¼ teaspoon salt
⅛ teaspoon white pepper
8 fl. oz. double cream [1 cup heavy
  cream]

Roll up the fillets Swiss [jelly] roll style
and secure with thread. Arrange the rolls
in a large ovenproof dish and set aside.

Strain the reserved mussel liquid
through a fine strainer set over a large
saucepan. Add the onion and bouquet
garni and pour over the wine. Set the pan
over high heat and bring the liquid to the
boil. Reduce the heat to low and simmer
the stock for 10 minutes. Remove the pan
from the heat and pour the stock through
a strainer set over a bowl. Discard the
contents of the strainer. Set aside.

Preheat the oven to moderate 350°F
(Gas Mark 4, 180°C).

In a large frying-pan, melt the butter

*Sole Normande, sole fillets garnished
with mussels and shrimps and a
creamy sauce, is a classic recipe.*

over moderate heat. When the foam
subsides, add the shallots, mushrooms,
lemon juice, salt and pepper to the pan.
Fry, stirring occasionally, for 5 minutes.
Transfer the mixture to the dish containing the fish rolls. Set the pan aside.

Add the mussels and shrimps to the
dish and pour over the reserved stock.
Place the dish in the oven and cook for
15 to 20 minutes or until the fish flesh
flakes easily when tested with a fork.
Remove the dish from the oven. Using a
slotted spoon, transfer the fish rolls to a
warmed serving dish. Remove and discard
the thread. Transfer the shallots, mushrooms, mussels and shrimps to the dish
and arrange them decoratively around
the fish. Keep hot.

Pour the cooking liquid through the
strainer into a large bowl. Discard the
contents of the strainer. Add the tablespoon of butter to the butter remaining
in the frying-pan. Place the pan over
moderate heat and melt the butter.
Remove the pan from the heat and, using
a wooden spoon, stir in the flour to make
a smooth paste. Gradually add the
reserved cooking liquid, stirring constantly. Stir in the salt and pepper and

return the pan to the heat. Cook the sauce, stirring constantly, for 2 to 3 minutes or until it is smooth and thick.

Stir in the cream. Pour the sauce over the fish and serve at once.

Sole Spanish-Style

☆ ☆   ① ① ① ✕ ✕

Most of the better known sole recipes are French in origin but the Mediterranean coast of Spain is deservedly noted for its seafood too, and the following method of cooking sole is equal in taste to any of the more complicated French dishes.

4 SERVINGS

4 globe artichokes
1½ teaspoons salt
2 soles, filleted
½ teaspoon white pepper
½ teaspoon lemon juice
8 fl. oz. [1 cup] dry white wine
1 oz. [2 tablespoons] butter
4 oz. mushrooms, thinly sliced
10 fl. oz. [1¼ cups] hot béchamel
  sauce

Prepare the artichokes for cooking by cutting off the stalks and removing the tough outer leaves. Trim the artichokes by cutting off the top points of the leaves.

Place the artichokes in a large saucepan and add enough water just to cover. Add ½ teaspoon of salt and place the pan over high heat. Bring the water to the boil, reduce the heat to moderate and cook the artichokes for 30 to 35 minutes, or until the bases are tender.

Meanwhile, season the sole fillets with the remaining salt, white pepper and lemon juice. Carefully roll up the fillets Swiss [jelly] roll style, securing them with a skewer or thread.

Place the fillets in a medium-sized saucepan and pour in the white wine. Place the pan over low heat and poach the fillets for 15 minutes, basting occasionally.

About 5 minutes before the artichokes and fish are cooked, prepare the mushrooms. In a frying-pan melt the butter over moderate heat. When the foam subsides, add the mushrooms and cook, stirring occasionally, for 3 minutes. Remove the pan from the heat.

Remove the artichokes from the heat and drain them on kitchen paper towels. Remove the choke and prickly leaves.

Arrange the artichokes on a serving dish. Spoon a little of the mushroom mixture into each cavity and cover with béchamel sauce.

With a slotted spoon, transfer the fish to a plate. Remove the skewers or thread and place one roll on top of each artichoke.

Serve immediately.

Sole Spanish-Style is sole served in succulent artichokes.

Sole Veronique

SOLE FILLETS WITH GRAPES

☆   ① ① ① ✕

Sole Veronique, the invention of a sauce chef at the Paris Ritz called Monsieur Malley, is a combination of fresh green grapes, wine sauce and delicately poached fish.

4 SERVINGS

1 oz. [2 tablespoons] plus 1 teaspoon
  butter
1 lb. Dover sole fillets, skinned and
  halved
½ teaspoon salt
1 teaspoon black pepper
1 large onion, thinly sliced
1 bay leaf, crumbled
8 fl. oz. [1 cup] dry white wine
2 fl. oz. [¼ cup] water
1 oz. [¼ cup] flour
4 fl. oz. [½ cup] milk
2 fl. oz. double cream [¼ cup heavy
  cream]
8 oz. green grapes, peeled, halved
  and seeded

Preheat the oven to moderate 350°F (Gas Mark 4, 180°C). With the teaspoon of butter, grease a large baking dish.

Rub the fish pieces with the salt and pepper and arrange them on the bottom of the baking dish.

Sprinkle over the onion and bay leaf and pour over the wine and water. Place the dish in the oven and cook for 15 to 20 minutes or until the fish flesh flakes easily when tested with a fork.

Remove the dish from the oven and, using a fish slice or slotted spoon, transfer the fish fillets to a warmed serving dish.

Strain the fish cooking liquid into a jug, pressing down on the onion to extract all the liquid. Reserve 4 fluid ounces [½ cup] of the stock.

In a small saucepan, melt the remaining butter over moderate heat. Remove the pan from the heat and, with a wooden spoon, stir in the flour to make a smooth paste. Gradually add the milk and the reserved stock, stirring constantly. Return the pan to the heat and cook, stirring constantly, for 2 to 3 minutes or until the sauce is thick and smooth. Stir in the cream and cook, stirring constantly, for a further 2 minutes.

Remove the pan from the heat and pour the sauce over the fillets. Arrange the grapes around the edge of the dish and serve immediately.

Trout with Almonds

Accompany this elegant dish with buttered French beans, boiled new potatoes and some well chilled Pouilly Fuissé wine.

6 SERVINGS

6 medium-sized trout, cleaned and with the eyes removed
1 teaspoon salt
1 teaspoon white pepper
2 tablespoons lemon juice
6 fl. oz. [¾ cup] milk
3 oz. [¾ cup] seasoned flour, made with 3 oz. [¾ cup] flour,
   1 teaspoon grated nutmeg and ¼ teaspoon dried thyme
5 oz. [⅝ cup] butter
4 oz. [1 cup] slivered almonds
6 lemon quarters

Place the fish on a working surface and rub them all over with the salt, pepper and 1 tablespoon of the lemon juice.

Place the milk in one shallow dish and the seasoned flour in another. Dip the trout, one by one, first in the milk then in the seasoned flour.

In a heavy-based frying-pan large enough to take the fish in one layer, melt 3 ounces [⅜ cup] of the butter over moderate heat. When the foam subsides, add the trout and fry them for 4 to 6 minutes on each side or until the flesh flakes easily. With a fish slice or spatula, transfer the trout to a warmed serving dish. Keep warm.

Add the remaining butter to the frying-pan. When the foam subsides, add the almonds and the remaining lemon juice and cook, stirring frequently, for 3 to 5 minutes or until the almonds are lightly browned. Remove the pan from the heat and pour the mixture over the trout.

Garnish the trout with the lemon quarters and serve at once.

Danish Fried Trout in Sour Cream Sauce

The sour cream and mushroom sauce which accompanies the fried trout in this recipe complements but does not overpower the delicate flavour of the fish. Serve with broccoli and new potatoes and accompany with a well-chilled white Moselle wine.

6 SERVINGS

3 oz. [¾ cup] seasoned flour, made with 3 oz. [¾ cup] flour, ½ teaspoon salt and ¼ teaspoon black pepper
6 medium-sized trout, cleaned and with the eyes removed
4 oz. [½ cup] butter
2 tablespoons vegetable oil

12 small button mushrooms, wiped clean and halved
½ teaspoon salt
¼ teaspoon freshly ground black pepper
1 teaspoon lemon juice
1 teaspoon paprika
10 fl. oz. [1¼ cups] sour cream
1 tablespoon finely chopped fresh parsley

Place the seasoned flour in a large, shallow dish. Dip the fish in the flour mixture, coating them completely and shaking off any excess. Set aside.

In a large saucepan, melt 2 ounces [¼ cup] of the butter with the oil over moderate heat. When the foam subsides, add the fish, 2 at a time, and fry them for 4 to 6 minutes on each side, or until they are lightly browned and the flesh flakes easily. Transfer the fish to a warmed serving dish and keep warm while you prepare the sauce.

Remove the saucepan from the heat and discard the cooking juices. Place the remaining butter in the pan and melt it over moderate heat. When the foam subsides, reduce the heat to low and, using a wooden spoon, scrape any sediment left on the bottom of the pan and incorporate it into the butter.

Add the mushrooms to the pan and cook, stirring occasionally, for 3 minutes. Add the salt, pepper, lemon juice, paprika and sour cream and, stirring constantly, cook for 2 to 3 minutes or until the mixture is hot but not boiling.

Remove the pan from the heat and pour the sauce over the fish. Sprinkle the parsley over the top and serve.

Trout in Tomato Sauce

This Italian method of baking trout makes an interesting alternative to the more traditional methods of cooking this superb fish.

4 SERVINGS

3 fl. oz. [⅜ cup] olive oil
1 garlic clove, crushed
2 lb. tomatoes, blanched, peeled, seeded and chopped
2 oz. [½ cup] seasoned flour, made with 2 oz. [½ cup] flour, ½ teaspoon salt and ¼ teaspoon black pepper
4 medium-sized trout, cleaned and with the eyes removed
1 tablespoon finely chopped

A delicious fish cooked in a simply delicious way — Danish Fried Trout in Sour Cream Sauce.

fresh parsley

In a saucepan, heat 2 tablespoons of the oil over moderate heat. When the oil is hot, add the garlic and cook for 2 minutes, stirring constantly. Add the tomatoes, reduce the heat to moderately low and simmer the tomato mixture, stirring occasionally, for 20 minutes.

Meanwhile, preheat the oven to moderate 350°F (Gas Mark 4, 180°C).

Place the seasoned flour in a large, shallow dish. Dip the fish into the flour

mixture, coating them thoroughly.

In a large, flameproof casserole, heat the remaining oil over moderate heat. When the oil is hot, add the fish and cook them for 2 minutes on each side, or until they are lightly browned all over.

Pour the tomato sauce over the trout and place the casserole in the oven. Bake for 10 to 15 minutes or until the fish flesh flakes easily when tested with a fork.

Remove from the oven, sprinkle over the chopped parsley and serve immediately.

Smoked Trout Pâté

☆ ⓵ ⓵ ⓵ ⧗

Simple and easy-to-make, Smoked Trout Pâté makes the perfect hors d'oeuvre, served with hot toast and butter.

6 SERVINGS

2 lb. smoked trout, skinned, boned and flaked
4 oz. single cream [½ cup light cream]
4 oz. cream cheese
2 tablespoons horseradish sauce
2 tablespoons lemon juice
1 teaspoon black pepper
1 tablespoon chopped fresh parsley

Place the fish and cream in the jar of an electric blender and blend at high speed until the mixture forms a purée.

Spoon the purée into a mixing bowl. Beat in the cream cheese, horseradish sauce, lemon juice, pepper and parsley. Continue beating until it is smooth and creamy. Spoon the pâté into individual ramekin dishes and smooth the top down with the back of a spoon.

Truro Skate with Egg and Lemon Sauce

Refreshing and light, Truro Skate with Egg and Lemon Sauce is delicious served with boiled potatoes and a crisp green salad.

6 SERVINGS
2 lb. skate wings, cleaned, trimmed and cut into large strips
2 pints [5 cups] fish stock
SAUCE
3 eggs, lightly beaten
juice of 4 lemons
½ teaspoon salt
¼ teaspoon black pepper
1 tablespoon chopped fresh parsley

Place the skate in a shallow saucepan. Pour over the stock and bring to the boil over moderate heat. Reduce the heat to low and simmer the fish for 15 to 20 minutes or until the fish flesh flakes easily.

Remove the pan from the heat and carefully transfer the skate to a warmed serving dish. Keep hot.

Discard all but 2 fluid ounces [¼ cup] of the cooking liquid. Place the eggs, lemon juice, salt, pepper and the reserved cooking liquid in a medium-sized heat-proof mixing bowl. Stir well to mix. Set the bowl in a saucepan half-filled with boiling water and place the saucepan over low heat. Cook the sauce, stirring constantly, for 5 to 6 minutes or until it is fairly thick and smooth.

Remove the pan from the heat and remove the bowl from the pan. Spoon the egg and lemon sauce over the fish, sprinkle over the parsley and serve.

Turbot with Orange

The delicacy of turbot is enhanced by marinating it in this mixture of orange and lemon juice. Serve with steamed broccoli and potatoes.

4 SERVINGS
4 turbot steaks
1 teaspoon salt
½ teaspoon black pepper
grated rind and juice of 2 oranges
grated rind and juice of 1 lemon
2 oz. [¼ cup] butter
1 orange, thinly sliced

Place the turbot steaks in a shallow flameproof casserole. Sprinkle over the salt and pepper, orange rind and juice

Two ways with turbot, Turbot with Orange, Turbot with Vegetable Rice.

and lemon rind and juice. Set aside to marinate at room temperature for 1 hour.

Preheat the grill [broiler] to high.

Cut the butter up into small pieces and dot over the fish. Place the dish under the grill [broiler] and grill [broil] for 5 to 8 minutes on each side or until the flesh flakes easily.

Remove the dish from under the heat. Using a fish slice, transfer the turbot steaks to a warmed serving dish. Garnish with the orange slices. Serve at once.

Turbot with Vegetable Rice

This classic French way of cooking turbot is a meal in itself.

4 SERVINGS
4 turbot steaks
1 teaspoon salt
½ teaspoon black pepper
2 garlic cloves, finely chopped
1 teaspoon dried rosemary
1 teaspoon dried marjoram
2 tablespoons chopped fresh parsley
8 fl. oz. [1 cup] fish stock
1 oz. [2 tablespoons] butter
1 onion, finely chopped
2 celery stalks, finely chopped
4 oz. mushrooms, sliced
12 oz. [2 cups] long-grain rice, washed, soaked in cold water for 30 minutes, drained, cooked and kept hot
2 large tomatoes, sliced

Preheat the oven to warm 325°F (Gas Mark 3, 170°C).

Place the turbot steaks on the bottom of a large ovenproof dish. Sprinkle over the salt, pepper, garlic, rosemary, marjoram and parsley. Pour over the stock. Place the dish in the centre of the oven and bake for 15 to 20 minutes or until the fish flesh flakes easily.

Meanwhile, prepare the rice. In a large frying-pan, melt the butter over moderate heat. When the foam subsides, add the onion, celery and mushrooms. Fry, stirring occasionally, for 5 to 7 minutes or until the onion is soft and translucent but not brown. Using a slotted spoon, transfer the vegetables to a large mixing bowl. Stir the rice into the mixture.

Add the tomato slices to the fat in the pan and fry them for 1 minute on each side. Remove the pan from the heat. Remove the turbot from the oven. Using a fish slice, transfer the turbot steaks to a warmed serving dish and arrange them around the edge. Discard the cooking liquid. Pile the rice mixture in the middle and garnish the turbot with the tomato slices. Serve at once.

Chiopino

A hearty fish stew from northern California, Chiopino should be served in bowls with hot French or garlic bread.

8-10 SERVINGS

4 fl. oz. [½ cup] olive oil
4 garlic cloves, finely chopped
1 tablespoon chopped parsley
1 celery stalk, chopped
1 green pepper, white pith removed, seeded and chopped
1 lb. tomatoes, blanched, peeled, seeded and coarsely chopped
8 oz. canned tomato purée
1 teaspoon salt
½ teaspoon black pepper
1 teaspoon paprika
8 fl. oz. [1 cup] red wine
½ teaspoon dried oregano
3 lb. white fish fillets, (haddock, cod, whiting, etc), skinned and cut into 1-inch pieces
1 lb. raw shrimps, shelled and deveined
4 oz. freshly cooked or canned crabmeat, shell and cartilage removed
24 mussels or clams, soaked, washed and scrubbed

In a large saucepan, heat the olive oil over moderate heat. Add the garlic, parsley, celery and green pepper and cook until they are lightly browned. Add the tomatoes, tomato purée, salt, pepper, paprika, wine and oregano and stir the ingredients well. Reduce the heat to low and simmer the sauce, covered, for 1 hour.

Add the white fish and shrimps to the sauce and increase the heat to moderate. Cook for 10 minutes, or until the fish and shrimps are tender. Stir in the crabmeat.

Meanwhile, put enough water into a saucepan to make a 1-inch layer on the bottom. Bring the water to the boil over moderate heat and put the mussels or clams in the pan. Cook for 6 to 8 minutes or until the shells open (be sure to discard any that do not open).

Turn the chiopino into a warmed serving dish and place the mussels or clams, in their shells, on top.

Serve immediately, giving each person a bowl for their discarded shells.

Russian Kulebiak

This traditional dish is fish and hard-boiled eggs wrapped in crisp, golden pastry. Accompany the pie with a jug of sour

cream and serve it with creamed potatoes and spinach for a really impressive dinner party dish.*

4-6 SERVINGS

PASTRY
6 oz. [1½ cups] flour
⅛ teaspoon salt
5 oz. [⅝ cup] butter, cut into small pieces
1 tablespoon vinegar
1 egg yolk
5 to 6 tablespoons iced water
FILLING
2 lb. cod, haddock or salmon
2 oz. [¼ cup] butter
1 onion, halved
1 carrot, scraped
1 celery stalk, trimmed and halved
bouquet garni consisting of 4 parsley sprigs, 1 thyme spray and 1 bay leaf tied together
2 fl. oz. [¼ cup] water
1 oz. [2 tablespoons] butter, melted
4 hard-boiled eggs, sliced
1 teaspoon salt
½ teaspoon black pepper
1 tablespoon chopped fresh parsley
1 egg, lightly beaten

First prepare the pastry. Sift the flour and salt into a mixing bowl. Mix the pieces of butter into the flour, using a knife. Add the vinegar, egg yolk and enough water to form the mixture into a firm dough, which should be lumpy.

Roll out the dough into an oblong shape. Fold it in three and turn it so that the open edges face you. Roll out again into an oblong shape and proceed as before. Repeat this once again to make three turns in all. Wrap the dough in greaseproof or waxed paper and put in the refrigerator to chill for 15 minutes.

Meanwhile, prepare the filling. Put the fish, butter, onion, carrot, celery, bouquet garni and water in a medium-sized saucepan. Set the pan over moderate heat and bring to the boil. Reduce the heat to low, cover the pan and simmer for 15 to 20 minutes, or until the fish flakes easily.

Remove the pan from the heat and carefully lift out the fish. Skin and bone the fish and flake it into small pieces.

Preheat the oven to fairly hot 400°F (Gas Mark 6, 200°C).

Remove the dough from the refrigerator and divide it in half. Roll each piece of dough into a rectangle, about 10 inches by 6 inches. Trim the edges and reserve the trimmings.

Carefully lift one piece of dough on to a baking sheet. Arrange the fish on the dough leaving a ¼-inch space around the sides of the dough. Pour the melted butter over the top. Cover with the hard-boiled eggs and sprinkle over the salt,

pepper and parsley.

Place the other piece of dough over the fish and eggs. Turn up the edges of the dough to make a shallow rim round the filling. Using your fingers, pinch the rim to seal the edges.

Cut two slits in the middle of the dough to allow the steam to escape. Roll out the trimmings and use to make a decoration for the top. Brush the dough with the beaten egg.

Place the pie in the oven and bake for 30 minutes, or until the pastry is golden brown.

Remove the sheet from the oven and transfer the fish-filled pastry to a warmed serving dish. Serve at once.

Mediterranean Fish Stew

This traditional Southern French dish is easy to prepare. It can be made with any type of white or oily fish fillets, or a mixture of the two, and is an excellent lunch or informal dinner party dish. Serve with lots of chilled Provençal white wine.

4-6 SERVINGS

1½ lb. fish fillets, boned
6 medium-sized potatoes, peeled and sliced
1 bay leaf
1 medium-sized onion, finely chopped
1 celery stalk, trimmed and chopped
2 garlic cloves, peeled and crushed plus 1 whole, peeled garlic clove
1 teaspoon salt
½ teaspoon black pepper
1 teaspoon chopped fresh fennel
1 teaspoon chopped fresh parsley
1 teaspoon finely grated orange rind
3 fl. oz. [⅜ cup] olive oil
boiling water
3 tablespoons alioli (garlic mayonnaise)
4 slices dry toasted French bread

Cut the fish into bite-sized pieces and arrange in the bottom of a large heavy saucepan. Cover with the potatoes. Add the bay leaf, onion, celery and crushed garlic. Sprinkle with salt, pepper, fennel, parsley and grated orange rind. Pour over the olive oil, then add just enough boiling water to cover. Cook the mixture over moderate heat for 20 minutes or until the potatoes are tender.

Strain the broth into another saucepan and put the fish and potatoes on a warmed serving dish. Just before serving the broth, remove the saucepan from the heat and, stirring constantly, very slowly add the alioli.

Place rounds of toast, well rubbed with

Simple Japanese Sardines may be eaten bones and all!

Red Caviar Dip

Red Caviar Dip is an impressive and delicious addition to any buffet spread. Provide thinly buttered rye bread or toast to eat with it.

6-8 SERVINGS

1 lb. cream cheese
2 hard-boiled eggs, finely chopped
1 shallot, finely chopped
1 garlic clove, crushed
4 fl. oz. single cream [½ cup light cream]
3 oz. red caviar
2 teaspoons lemon juice

Place the cream cheese, eggs, shallot and garlic in a bowl. Beat the mixture until it is creamy. Stir in the cream and continue mixing until all the ingredients are thoroughly combined. Stir in the caviar and lemon juice.

Spoon the mixture into a serving bowl and place it in the refrigerator to chill for 30 minutes before serving.

Japanese Sardines

Sardines cooked in the Japanese style, flavoured with ginger and garlic, these can be eaten whole, bones and all. They make a delicious, unusual hors d'oeuvre served with brown bread and butter.

4 SERVINGS

4 fl. oz. [½ cup] soy sauce
2 fl. oz. [¼ cup] vinegar
2 tablespoons lemon juice
1 oz. fresh root ginger, peeled and chopped
2 garlic cloves, crushed
1 lb. fresh sardines, washed thoroughly in cold water and dried

2 tablespoons olive oil

In a small mixing bowl, combine the soy sauce, vinegar, lemon juice, ginger and garlic.

Arrange the sardines in a shallow baking dish and pour the soy sauce mixture over them. Leave the sardines in a cool place to marinate for 2 hours, basting them occasionally.

Preheat the grill [broiler] to high.

Remove the sardines from the marinade. Discard the marinade and dry the fish on kitchen paper towels. Reduce the heat of the grill [broiler] to moderate.

Line the grill [broiler] pan with aluminium foil. Brush the foil with half the oil. Place the sardines on the foil and brush them with the remaining oil.

Cook the sardines for 3 to 5 minutes or longer, depending on the size of the sardines, turning them once so that they are brown on both sides.

Remove the fish from the grill [broiler] and serve immediately.

53

Crabmeat and Avocado Mousse

This delicately flavoured, attractive mousse makes the perfect fish course for a dinner party. Or serve it as a light summer lunch with a mixed salad and garlic bread.

4-6 SERVINGS

1 teaspoon vegetable oil
3 large avocados, halved, stoned, peeled and chopped
2 tablespoons mayonnaise
1 teaspoon lemon juice
2 hard-boiled eggs, chopped
½ teaspoon salt
¼ teaspoon black pepper
4 spring onions [scallions], trimmed and chopped
¾ oz. gelatine, dissolved in 4 tablespoons hot water
4 oz. canned and drained or frozen and thawed crabmeat, shell and cartilage removed
4 fl. oz. double cream [½ cup heavy cream]
½ teaspoon curry powder

Using the teaspoon of vegetable oil, grease a 1-pint [1-quart] mould and set it aside.

Place the avocados, mayonnaise, lemon juice, eggs, salt, pepper, spring onions [scallions] and 3 tablespoons of the gelatine mixture in the jar of an electric blender. Blend at high speed for 30 seconds or until the mixture forms a smooth purée.

Pour half of the purée into the prepared mould and smooth over the top with the

back of a spoon. Chill the mould in the refrigerator for 15 minutes.

Meanwhile, in a medium-sized mixing bowl, combine the remaining gelatine with the crabmeat, cream and curry powder, beating with a wooden spoon until the mixture is well blended and smooth.

Remove the mould from the refrigerator and spoon over the crabmeat mixture, smoothing it over with the back of the spoon. Chill the mould in the refrigerator for 15 minutes. Spoon over the remaining avocado mixture and smooth over the top. Chill the mixture in the refrigerator for a further 4 hours.

To unmould the mousse, run a sharp knife around the edge of the mould to loosen the sides. Quickly dip the bottom of the mould in boiling water. Hold a chilled serving plate, inverted, over the mould and reverse the two, giving the mould a sharp shake. The mousse should slide out easily.

Serve immediately.

Crabmeat Flan

This rich flan may be served hot or cold as an hors d'oeuvre. Accompanied by a tossed salad, it also makes a light but appetizing main dish. A well-chilled white Loire wine, Pouilly Fumé for instance, would go well with it.

6-8 SERVINGS

FILLING
1 lb. crabmeat, fresh or canned
1 teaspoon lemon juice

Creamy, filling Crabmeat Flan makes a perfect dish for informal entertaining.

1 tablespoon chopped fennel leaves
1 small onion, finely chopped
2 tablespoons chopped parsley
2 tablespoons dry sherry
4 eggs, lightly beaten
12 fl. oz. single cream [1½ cups light cream]
¼ teaspoon ground cinnamon
½ teaspoon salt
¼ teaspoon white pepper
PASTRY
6 oz. [1½ cups] flour
2 teaspoons castor sugar
¼ teaspoon salt
1½ oz. [3 tablespoons] butter
1½ oz. [3 tablespoons] vegetable fat
1 to 2 tablespoons iced water

Remove any shell and cartilage from the crabmeat.

In a large mixing bowl, combine the crabmeat, lemon juice, fennel, onion, parsley and sherry together. Cover the bowl and place it in the refrigerator to chill for 1 hour.

Meanwhile to make the pastry, sift the flour, sugar and salt into a medium-sized mixing bowl. Add the butter and vegetable fat and cut them into small pieces with a table knife. With your fingertips, rub the fat into the flour until the mixture resembles fine breadcrumbs.

Add 1 tablespoon of iced water and, using a knife, mix it into the flour mixture. With your hands, mix and knead the

Crabmeat Salad, with its unusual, tangy rémoulade salad dressing, is an ideal summer buffet dish.

dough until it is smooth. Add more water if the dough is too dry. Chill the dough in the refrigerator for 30 minutes.

Preheat the oven to hot 425°F (Gas Mark 7, 220°C).

Roll out the dough ¼-inch thick. Lift the dough on your rolling pin and lay it over a 9-inch pie dish or 12-inch flan ring. Ease the dough into the dish and trim the edges with a sharp knife. Place the pastry shell in the oven and bake 'blind' for 15 minutes.

Remove the pie dish or flan ring from the oven and spoon the crab mixture into the pastry shell, spreading it out evenly.

In a large mixing bowl, combine the eggs, cream, cinnamon, salt and pepper together using a wooden spoon. Strain the mixture over the crab mixture in the pastry shell.

Place the flan in the oven and bake for 10 minutes.

Reduce the heat to moderate 350°F (Gas Mark 4, 180°C) and continue baking for 1 hour, or until a knife inserted into the centre of the flan comes out clean.

Remove the flan from the oven and serve at once if you are serving it hot.

Crabmeat Salad

The tangy rémoulade dressing adds a delicious finishing touch to this colourful and very rich summer salad. Serve as a luxurious lunch or buffet supper with some chilled rosé wine.

4 SERVINGS

MAYONNAISE

2 egg yolks, at room temperature
½ teaspoon salt
¾ teaspoon dry mustard
⅛ teaspoon cayenne pepper
8 fl. oz. [1 cup] olive oil, at room temperature
1 teaspoon white wine vinegar or lemon juice

REMOULADE SAUCE

1 teaspoon anchovy essence
½ teaspoon finely chopped fresh parsley
½ tablespoon capers (optional)
1 hard-boiled egg, chopped
1 garlic clove, crushed
1 teaspoon chopped fresh tarragon or ½ teaspoon dried tarragon

SALAD

1 lb. cooked crabmeat, fresh or canned
1 large Webb [iceberg] lettuce washed, outer leaves removed and separated into leaves
4 firm tomatoes, sliced

1 avocado, peeled, stoned, sliced and gently rubbed with lemon juice
½ cucumber, thinly sliced
9 black olives, stoned

To prepare the mayonnaise, in a medium-sized mixing bowl, combine the egg yolks, salt, mustard and cayenne with a wire whisk. Add the oil, a few drops at a time, whisking constantly. Do not add the oil too quickly or the mayonnaise will curdle. When the mayonnaise is thick, the oil may be added more quickly. As you are adding the oil, beat in a few drops of vinegar or lemon juice from time to time to prevent the mayonnaise from becoming too thick. When all the oil has been added, add the remaining vinegar or lemon juice. Taste for seasoning and add more salt and mustard, if desired.

In a large mixing bowl, combine the mayonnaise with all the other ingredients for the rémoulade sauce and mix thoroughly.

Remove any shell and cartilage from the crabmeat.

Arrange the lettuce leaves on a large serving dish. Put the crabmeat in the centre of the dish and arrange the tomatoes, avocado, cucumber and olives around the crabmeat.

Pour the dressing over the top and serve immediately.

Luxurious Lobster Bouchées are small pastry cases enclosing a rich, creamy lobster, mushrooms, cream and sherry filling. Serve them as a very special appetizer or first course to a fairly light meal.

Homard à l'Americaine

LOBSTER COOKED WITH GARLIC, HERBS, TOMATOES AND WINE

A famous lobster dish, Homard à l'Americaine is said to have originated in France, but it was first served, in its present form, in New York in 1860. It looks most attractive served in a ring of rice, accompanied by a fresh green salad and a well chilled Pouilly Fumé.

4 SERVINGS

2 x 2 lb. cooked lobsters, shells split, claws cracked and grey sac removed
1 oz. [2 tablespoons] butter
2 tablespoons olive oil
2 shallots, peeled and finely chopped
1 garlic clove, chopped
6 tomatoes, blanched, peeled, seeded and chopped
1 tablespoon chopped fresh tarragon or ½ tablespoon dried tarragon
2 tablespoons chopped fresh parsley
2 teaspoons chopped fresh thyme or 1 teaspoon dried thyme
8 fl. oz. [1 cup] dry white wine
½ teaspoon salt
¼ teaspoon freshly ground black pepper
⅛ teaspoon cayenne pepper
2 fl. oz. [¼ cup] brandy

Remove the lobster meat from the shells and claws and cut it into 2-inch pieces. Set aside.

In a large frying-pan, melt the butter with the oil over moderate heat. When the foam subsides, add the shallots and garlic and fry, stirring occasionally, for 3 to 4 minutes, or until the shallots are golden brown.

Add the tomatoes, tarragon, parsley, thyme, wine, salt, pepper and cayenne. Bring to the boil, reduce the heat to moderately low and simmer the mixture for 20 minutes.

Add the lobster pieces to the pan.

In a small saucepan, warm the brandy over low heat until it is hot. Remove the pan from the heat and ignite the brandy. Carefully pour it, still flaming, into the frying-pan.

Cook the mixture for a further 5

minutes, to heat the lobster through thoroughly.

Remove the frying-pan from the heat and transfer the lobster and its sauce to a large, warmed serving dish. Serve at once.

Lobster Bouchées

Lobster Bouchées, with a superb creamy filling, make a delicious hors d'oeuvre or cocktail bites. They are very rich and filling, however, so try not to serve them when you have a rather heavy main course planned to follow.

18 SMALL BOUCHEES

18 small frozen bouchée cases, thawed, baked and kept hot
FILLING
1 x 2 lb. cooked lobster, shell split, claws cracked and grey sac removed
1 oz. [2 tablespoons] butter
8 oz. mushrooms, wiped clean and sliced
2 egg yolks
2 tablespoons double [heavy] cream
10 fl. oz. [1¼ cups] béchamel sauce
½ teaspoon salt
½ teaspoon freshly ground black pepper
⅛ teaspoon cayenne pepper
4 fl. oz. [½ cup] medium-dry sherry

2 teaspoons lemon juice

To make the filling, remove the lobster meat from the shells and claws. Discard the shells and cut the meat into dice. Set aside.

In a medium-sized frying-pan, melt the butter over moderate heat. When the foam subsides, add the mushrooms and cook, stirring occasionally, for 4 to 6 minutes or until they are tender. With a slotted spoon, remove the mushrooms from the pan and set them aside on a plate.

In a small mixing bowl, beat the egg yolks and cream together with a wire whisk or rotary beater until they are blended. Set aside.

In a medium-sized saucepan, heat the béchamel sauce over moderate heat. Add the diced lobster, mushrooms, salt, pepper and cayenne. Stirring carefully, cook the sauce for 2 to 3 minutes. Do not worry if the sauce is quite thick at this stage.

Remove the pan from the heat. Carefully stir in the egg yolk and cream mixture. Return the pan to low heat and, stirring constantly, cook the sauce gently for 2 minutes. Stir in the sherry and lemon juice and cook for 1 minute. Taste the sauce and add more seasoning if necessary.

Spoon a little of the filling into each of the hot bouchée cases, carefully transfer them to an attractive serving dish and serve them at once.

Lobster with Brandy Sauce

☆ ① ① ① ⌛

This superb dish, flavoured with brandy and cayenne, makes an ideal first course to a lunch or dinner party. Or, alternatively, it may be served as a light luncheon with creamed potatoes.

2-4 SERVINGS

1 x 3 lb. cooked lobster, shell split, claws cracked and grey sac removed
1½ oz. [3 tablespoons] butter
2 teaspoons olive oil
½ teaspoon salt
¼ teaspoon freshly ground black pepper
¼ teaspoon cayenne pepper
6 fl. oz. [¾ cup] brandy
2 teaspoons cornflour [cornstarch] mixed with 2 tablespoons water

Lobster with Brandy Sauce is down-right extravagant to make - but the spectacular results are more than worth the initial expense.

Remove the lobster meat from the shell, cut it into small pieces and set aside. Wipe the shell halves clean and place them in a heatproof dish with the claws. Set the dish aside.

In a medium-sized frying-pan, melt the butter with the oil over moderate heat. When the foam subsides, add the lobster meat, salt, pepper and cayenne and fry, stirring occasionally, for 3 to 4 minutes, or until the lobster meat is lightly browned.

Preheat the grill [broiler] to moderate.

In a small saucepan, heat the brandy over low heat until it is hot but not boil-

ing. Remove the pan from the heat and carefully pour the brandy over the lobster meat. Ignite the brandy with a match and leave it until the flames have completely died down.

With a slotted spoon, remove the lobster meat from the pan and place it in the reserved shell halves.

Place the pan over moderate heat and bring the liquid to the boil. Reduce the heat to low and stir in the cornflour [cornstarch] mixture, a little at a time, beating constantly until the ingredients are blended and the sauce has thickened. Remove the pan from the heat and pour the sauce over the lobster meat.

Place the dish under the grill [broiler] and grill [broil] for about 5 minutes or until the lobster is golden brown.

Remove from the grill [broiler] and serve at once.

Oyster Chowder

☆ ① ① ① ✕

A warming mixture of oysters, vegetables and cream, Oyster Chowder makes a delicious light lunch or supper served with hot buttered toast.

4-6 SERVINGS

1½ oz. [3 tablespoons] butter
1 large onion, finely chopped
2 celery stalks, trimmed and chopped
1 medium-sized carrot, scraped and chopped
2 medium-sized potatoes, peeled and diced
4 fl. oz. [½ cup] boiling water
1½ teaspoons salt
32 fresh oysters, shelled and with the oyster liquid reserved
½ teaspoon black pepper
10 fl. oz. single cream [1¼ cups light cream]
1 tablespoon chopped fresh parsley

In a large saucepan, melt 1 ounce [2 tablespoons] of the butter over moderate heat. When the foam subsides, add the onion and celery to the pan and fry, stirring occasionally, for 5 to 7 minutes or until the onion is soft and translucent but not brown. Add the carrot and potatoes. Pour over the water and add ½ teaspoon of the salt.

Increase the heat to high and bring the liquid back to the boil. Reduce the heat to low, cover the pan and cook for 15 minutes, or until the potatoes and carrot are tender.

Meanwhile, in a second large saucepan, melt the remaining butter over moderate heat. When the foam subsides, add the oysters and their liquid. Cover the pan and cook the oysters for 2 minutes. Remove the pan from the heat and set aside.

When the potatoes and carrot are cooked, add the remaining salt, the pepper and the cream. Pour in the cooked oysters and their liquid. Cook the chowder, stirring frequently, for a further 2 minutes, or until it is hot but not boiling.

Taste the chowder and add more salt and pepper if necessary.

Remove the pan from the heat. Ladle the chowder into a warmed tureen. Sprinkle with the parsley and serve immediately.

Marinated Oysters is an exquisite dish of fresh oysters marinated in wine, oil and lemon juice.

Oyster Cocktail

☆ ① ① ① ✕

Oysters in a piquant sauce resting on a bed of crisp lettuce leaves, Oyster Cocktail makes a tasty start to a meal.

4 SERVINGS

2 tablespoons tomato purée
1 teaspoon Worcestershire sauce
1 tablespoon fresh lemon juice
¼ teaspoon salt
⅛ teaspoon black pepper
5 fl. oz. double cream [⅝ cup heavy cream]
16 fresh oysters, shelled
1 small crisp lettuce, outer leaves removed, washed and separated into leaves
1 lemon, sliced
½ small cucumber, sliced

In a large mixing bowl, combine the tomato purée, Worcestershire sauce, lemon juice, salt and pepper with a fork. Add the cream and beat the mixture well to combine all the ingredients. Stir in the oysters, coating them thoroughly with the sauce.

Line 4 individual serving glasses with the lettuce leaves. Spoon equal amounts of the oyster mixture on to the lettuce

leaves. Garnish each serving with lemon and cucumber slices.

Place the glasses in the refrigerator and chill for 30 minutes before serving.

Oysters with Cream and Cheese

A deliciously tempting first course for a dinner party, Oysters with Cream and Cheese is surprisingly quick and easy to make — and the reward, with this elegant dish, is readily apparent. Canned oysters have been used in this recipe because they are usually more available than fresh. If you do have access to fresh oysters, however, the dish is of course even more superb! Remove them from their shells and cook them first.

4 SERVINGS

2 oz. [¼ cup] plus 1 teaspoon butter, melted
16 canned oysters, drained
6 fl. oz. double cream [¾ cup heavy cream]
2 oz. [½ cup] Parmesan cheese, grated

Preheat the grill [broiler] to moderately high. With the teaspoon of butter, lightly grease a medium-sized shallow, flame-proof baking dish.

Place the oysters, in one layer, in the baking dish. Spoon a little of the cream over each one, then sprinkle generously with grated cheese. Spoon a little of the remaining melted butter on top of each oyster and place the dish under the grill [broiler]. Cook the oysters for 3 to 5 minutes, or until the topping bubbles slightly and has browned.

Remove the dish from the grill [broiler] and serve the oysters at once.

Marinated Oysters

This exquisitely simple first course is a delectable combination of fresh oysters, white wine, lemon juice and herbs, served cold. It makes an elegant start to a dinner party although, since it is quite rich and filling, it is best followed by a light main course. Serve with small squares of brown bread and butter and a well-chilled white Chablis wine.

4 SERVINGS

16 fresh oysters
MARINADE
6 fl. oz. [¾ cup] dry white wine
2 fl. oz. [¼ cup] olive oil
2 fl. oz. [¼ cup] lemon juice
¼ teaspoon salt

¼ teaspoon black pepper
¼ teaspoon dried thyme
¼ teaspoon dried chervil
1 teaspoon chopped fresh parsley
1 garlic clove, crushed

First, prepare the marinade. In a large mixing bowl, combine all the marinade ingredients, stirring with a fork or spoon to blend well. Set aside for 15 minutes.

Meanwhile, detach the oysters from their shells and place them in a medium-sized saucepan. Discard the shells.

Add the marinade to the oysters and place the pan over moderate heat. Bring the liquid to the boil, then remove the pan from the heat.

Transfer the oysters and liquid to a medium-sized serving bowl and set aside to cool to room temperature.

Serve the oysters cold, in their marinade.

Oysters Rockefeller

A delicious appetizer, Oysters Rockefeller is an adaptation of a well-known American

Oysters Rockefeller is a classic American hors d'oeuvre.

recipe which originated in New Orleans.

4 SERVINGS

sufficient rock salt to cover the bottom of 2 large baking dishes in a layer about ½-inch thick
4 spring onions [scallions], chopped
2 celery stalks, finely chopped
8 oz. cooked spinach
3 parsley sprigs
1 teaspoon salt
¼ teaspoon black pepper
¼ teaspoon cayenne pepper
2 fl. oz. single cream [¼ cup light cream]
1 tablespoon Pernod
36 fresh oysters, one shell removed

Preheat the oven to very hot 450°F (Gas Mark 8, 230°C).

Cover the bottom of two large baking dishes with the rock salt. Set aside.

Place the spring onions [scallions], celery, spinach, parsley, salt, pepper, cayenne and cream in an electric blender and blend, off and on, for 2 minutes or until the ingredients are puréed. Transfer the purée to a mixing bowl. Add the Pernod and stir well. Divide the oysters equally between the baking dishes. Cover each one with a teaspoonful of the purée. Place the baking dishes in the oven and bake for 4 minutes.

Remove the baking dishes from the oven and serve immediately.

59

Coquilles St.-Jacques à la Crème

SCALLOPS IN CREAM SAUCE

A superbly elegant first course to serve for a dinner party, Coquilles St.-Jacques à la Crème takes very little time to prepare.

4 SERVINGS

4 fl. oz. [½ cup] white wine
½ teaspoon lemon juice
1 lb. scallops
1 tablespoon butter
2 tablespoons flour
5 fl. oz. single cream [⅝ cup light cream]
¼ teaspoon salt
¼ teaspoon black pepper
⅛ teaspoon cayenne pepper
red food colouring
1 oz. [¼ cup] Gruyère cheese, grated

In a heavy, medium-sized saucepan heat the wine and lemon juice over moderate heat. When the liquid boils, reduce the heat to moderately low and drop the scallops into the pan. Simmer them gently for 8 to 10 minutes or until they are firm. Remove the pan from the heat and place to one side to cool.

When the liquid has cooled, strain it into a bowl or jug. With a sharp knife, slice the scallops in half and set them aside. In a medium-sized heavy saucepan, melt the butter over low heat. Remove the pan from the heat and, with a wooden spoon, stir in the flour. Gradually add the liquid from cooking the scallops to the pan, stirring constantly. Return the pan to moderate heat and bring the sauce to the boil. Stirring constantly, cook the sauce for 3 minutes. Stir in the cream, salt, pepper, cayenne and a few drops of red food colouring as liked, and cook for a further 2 minutes. Fold the scallops into the sauce.

Preheat the grill [broiler] to moderate.

Spoon the scallops and sauce into four large scallop shells or individual cocotte dishes. Sprinkle the grated cheese over the tops and brown under the grill [broiler] for 4 to 5 minutes. Serve.

Coquilles St-Jacques Gratinées

SCALLOPS AND MUSHROOMS IN WHITE WINE SAUCE AND CHEESE

This mouthwatering main dish may be served with puréed potatoes, buttered peas or broccoli.

4 SERVINGS

1 tablespoon butter
1½ lb. scallops, sliced
6 fl. oz. [¾ cup] dry white wine
4 oz. mushrooms, sliced
½ teaspoon salt
6 peppercorns
1 bay leaf
3 parsley sprigs
2 shallots, finely minced
2 fl. oz. [¼ cup] water
SAUCE
2½ oz. [¼ cup plus 1 tablespoon] butter
4 tablespoons flour
6 fl. oz. [¾ cup] milk
2 egg yolks
4 fl. oz. double cream [½ cup heavy cream]
¼ teaspoon salt
⅛ teaspoon white pepper
¼ teaspoon grated nutmeg
1 teaspoon lemon juice
2 oz. [½ cup] Gruyère cheese, grated
1 tablespoon melted butter

With the butter, grease 4 shallop shells or a medium-sized flameproof serving dish.

Put the scallops in a medium-sized saucepan and add the wine, mushrooms, salt, peppercorns, bay leaf, parsley and shallots. The scallops should be almost covered so if necessary, add the water. Heat the liquid to boiling point over moderate heat, cover and cook the scallops for 5 minutes. Remove the scallops and mushrooms from the liquid and put them in a bowl to one side.

Increase the heat to high and boil the liquid in the saucepan until it is reduced by about one-third. Pour the liquid through a strainer into a jug.

Preheat the grill [broiler] to moderate.

To make the sauce, in a small saucepan, melt the butter over low heat. Remove the pan from the heat and, with a wooden spoon, stir in the flour. Gradually stir in 6 fluid ounces [¾ cup] of the reduced scallop cooking liquid. Return the pan to the heat and bring to the boil. Cook, stirring constantly, for 5 minutes or until the sauce is thick and smooth. Lightly beat in the milk and cook, stirring, for a further 1 minute. Remove the pan from the heat and place to one side.

Put the egg yolks in a small bowl with the cream and beat with a fork to mix. Stirring constantly, add a little hot sauce to the beaten egg yolks and cream. Stir the mixture into the remaining sauce in the pan and return the pan to the heat. Heat the sauce gently, stirring, and remove the pan from the heat. Add the salt, pepper, nutmeg and lemon juice. Fold the scallops and mushrooms into the sauce.

Spoon the scallop mixture into the shells or dish. Sprinkle the grated cheese and the melted butter over the tops of each shell or over the dish. Brown under the grill [broiler] for 6 minutes or until the cheese has melted and is brown and sizzling. Serve immediately.

Scallop Salad

A colourful and appetizing dish, Scallop Salad makes a delightful meal to serve at an informal dinner party. Serve with garlic bread and a well-chilled white wine, such as Graves.

4-6 SERVINGS

16 scallops, poached, drained and halved
12 mussels, scrubbed, steamed and removed from their shells
6 oz. prawns or shrimps, shelled and deveined
1 small head of fennel, trimmed and thinly sliced
2 medium-sized green peppers, white pith removed, seeded and sliced
8 oz. green beans, cooked, drained and cut into 1-inch lengths
6 medium-sized tomatoes, quartered
12 small new potatoes, boiled, drained and peeled
6 spring onions [scallions], trimmed and cut into 1-inch lengths
1 medium-sized cucumber, roughly diced
12 stoned black olives
DRESSING
2 garlic cloves, crushed
1 teaspoon prepared French mustard
2 teaspoons sugar
½ teaspoon salt
½ teaspoon black pepper
2 teaspoons chopped fresh basil or 1 teaspoon dried basil
6 fl. oz. [¾ cup] olive oil
2 fl. oz. [¼ cup] white wine vinegar

First prepare the dressing. In a medium-sized bowl, combine the garlic, mustard, sugar, salt, pepper and basil. Gradually beat in the olive oil and vinegar until the mixture is thoroughly combined. Set aside.

In a large salad bowl, combine the scallops, mussels, prawns or shrimps, fennel, peppers, beans, tomatoes, potatoes, spring onions [scallions], cucumber and black olives. Pour the dressing over the salad and, using two large spoons, toss the salad until the ingredients are coated with the dressing. Serve immediately.

Refreshing Scallop Salad.

Stir-fried Abalone and Chinese Cabbage

 ①

This unusual dish of Chinese cabbage, abalone and leek, flavoured with soy sauce, ginger and lemon juice (pictured on page 33) may be served as part of a Chinese meal, or as a light lunch with boiled rice or noodles.

4 SERVINGS

3 tablespoons peanut oil
½-inch piece fresh root ginger, peeled and very thinly sliced
1 small leek, white part only, thinly sliced and pushed out into rings
1 small Chinese cabbage, coarse outer leaves removed, washed and shredded
⅛ teaspoon monosodium glutamate (optional)
½ teaspoon salt
¼ teaspoon white pepper
2 teaspoons soy sauce
1½ tablespoons fresh lemon juice
14 oz. canned abalone, drained and sliced

In a large frying-pan, heat the oil over moderate heat. When the oil is hot, add the ginger and leek and stir-fry for 2 minutes. Add the cabbage and stir-fry for 4 minutes, or until the cabbage is cooked but still crisp.

Sprinkle over the monosodium glutamate (if you are using it), salt, pepper, soy sauce and lemon juice. Stir in the sliced abalone and cook the mixture, stirring constantly, for 5 minutes.

Remove the pan from the heat. Turn the mixture into a warmed serving dish and serve immediately.

Clams Marinara

 ① ①

Clams Marinara is clams steamed in white wine and covered with a sauce of tomatoes, onion and garlic. If clams are not available small oysters or cockles can be substituted. This dish may be served as a main course with buttered rice, and a mixed salad. Serve with crusty rolls or French bread.

4 SERVINGS

2 hard-boiled eggs
3 tablespoons olive oil
1 large onion, chopped
2 garlic cloves, crushed
1½ oz. [¾ cup] fresh white breadcrumbs
1½ lb. tomatoes, blanched, peeled and chopped
½ teaspoon salt
¼ teaspoon black pepper

4 dozen small fresh clams, in shells
15 fl. oz. [1⅞ cups] white wine
2 tablespoons chopped fresh parsley
2 lemons, cut in wedges

Separate the egg whites from the yolks. Chop the whites into small pieces. Press the yolks through a strainer or, if you have one, a garlic crusher. Set aside.

In a medium-sized frying-pan, heat the oil over moderate heat. Add the onion and garlic and fry, stirring occasionally, for 5 to 7 minutes or until the onion is soft and translucent but not brown. Add the breadcrumbs, tomatoes, egg yolks, salt and pepper. Stir and mash with the back of a wooden spoon until the mixture becomes a smooth, thick purée. Set aside.

Place the clams in a heavy pot. Pour the wine over them and bring to the boil. Cover, reduce the heat and simmer for 10 minutes or until the clams open. Throw away any clams that have remained closed.

Place the clams in a deep, heated serving dish. Strain the liquid from the pan and add to the purée. Taste and adjust seasoning by adding more salt and pepper if necessary. Pour the sauce over the clams. Sprinkle with parsley and the egg whites and serve immediately. The lemon wedges should be served on a separate dish.

Paella

 ① ① ①

You may vary the ingredients in Paella using tiny eels and prawns or shrimps instead of the combination suggested here. Rabbit may be substituted for the chicken.

6-8 SERVINGS

1 lobster, shell split, claws cracked and grey sac removed
3 fl. oz. [⅜ cup] olive oil
1 x 3 lb. chicken, cut into 12 serving pieces
6 lean bacon slices, chopped
2 large tomatoes, blanched, peeled, seeded and chopped
2 garlic cloves, finely chopped
8 oz. mange-tout, washed
1 lb. [2⅔ cups] long-grain rice, washed, soaked in cold water for 30 minutes and drained
2 teaspoons paprika
2 pints [5 cups] water
2 teaspoons salt
¼ teaspoon ground saffron
12 small clams, steamed
6 snails
8 oz. baby squid, cleaned
6 lemon wedges

Remove the lobster meat from the shell

and claws and cut it into 1-inch pieces.

In a large flameproof casserole, heat the olive oil over moderate heat. When it is hot, add the chicken pieces and the bacon and fry, turning occasionally, for 5 to 8 minutes or until the chicken pieces are lightly browned. Add the tomatoes, garlic and mange-tout and fry for a further 5 minutes, stirring frequently.

Using a slotted spoon, remove the mixture from the casserole. Set aside.

Add the rice and paprika to the casserole and, shaking it frequently, cook for 3 minutes or until the rice is well coated with the oil. Add the water, salt and saffron, stir and bring to the boil. Reduce the heat to low, add the chicken and vegetable mixture and cook for 10 minutes, stirring occasionally. Add the clams, snails, squid and lobster and cook for a further 5 to 10 minutes or until the chicken is cooked through and all the liquid has been absorbed by the rice.

Remove the casserole from the heat. Serve, garnished with the lemon wedges.

Shrimp and Avocado Surprise

 ① ①

An unusual appetizing dish which is both easy to make and impressive to serve, Shrimp and Avocado Surprise may be accompanied by melba toast and butter.

6 SERVINGS

3 ripe avocados, halved and stoned
10 oz. frozen peeled shrimps, thawed and drained
5 fl. oz. [⅝ cup] mayonnaise
2 garlic cloves, crushed
1 teaspoon ground coriander
¼ teaspoon grated nutmeg
1 teaspoon salt
½ teaspoon black pepper
juice of ½ lemon
6 slices streaky bacon, rinds removed, grilled [broiled] until very crisp and crumbled

Using a teaspoon, scoop out the avocado flesh, leaving the skins intact. Set the skins aside.

Place the avocado flesh in a medium-sized mixing bowl. Mash the flesh with a fork until it is smooth and creamy. Add the shrimps, mayonnaise, garlic, coriander, nutmeg, salt, pepper and lemon juice. With a wooden spoon, stir the ingredients until they are well blended.

Spoon the avocado mixture back into the reserved avocado skins. Sprinkle over the crumbled bacon and serve.

Classic Paella from Spain.

Shrimp Egg Foo Yung

This Chinese omelet makes a delightful first course for a dinner party, or it may be served as part of a Chinese meal.

4 SERVINGS

3 tablespoons vegetable oil
8 oz. shrimps, chopped
4 oz. mushrooms, sliced
4 oz. bean sprouts, washed
4 eggs, lightly beaten

SAUCE

8 fl. oz. [1 cup] chicken stock
2 teaspoons soy sauce
¼ teaspoon salt
1 tablespoon cornflour [cornstarch]
  mixed with 1 tablespoon water

In a frying-pan, heat 1 tablespoon of the oil over moderate heat. When the oil is hot, add the shrimps to the pan and stir-fry for 3 minutes or until they are heated through. Remove from the heat and set aside.

To make the sauce, in a small saucepan, bring the stock, soy sauce, salt and cornflour [cornstarch] mixture to the boil over moderate heat, stirring constantly. Cook the sauce for 1 minute, or until it has thickened slightly. Set aside.

In a mixing bowl, combine the mush-rooms, bean sprouts, eggs and shrimps and beat them together with a fork.

Return the frying-pan to moderate heat. Add the remaining oil to the pan. When the oil is hot, add a quarter of the egg mixture and cook it for 1 minute or until the bottom is set and golden brown. Using a spatula or palette knife, turn the omelet over and cook for a further 1 minute or until it is just set. Transfer the omelet to a serving dish and keep warm. Cook the remaining egg mixture in the same way, to make 3 more omelets.

Return the pan to moderate heat and bring the sauce to the boil, stirring. Remove the pan from the heat and pour a little of the sauce over the omelets. Serve immediately.

Squid in Red Wine

This economical recipe makes an unusual but festive supper dish.

4 SERVINGS

2½ lb. squid, cleaned and skinned
4 tablespoons olive oil
2 medium-sized onions, sliced
2 garlic cloves, crushed
5 fl. oz. [⅝ cup] red wine
½ teaspoon salt

Delicate Shrimp Egg Foo Yung.

½ teaspoon black pepper
1 teaspoon dried oregano
½ teaspoon fennel seeds
¼ teaspoon dried marjoram
6 large tomatoes, blanched, peeled,
  seeded and chopped
1 teaspoon dried basil

Cut the squid into ¼-inch slices and chop the tentacles.

In a flameproof casserole, heat half the oil over moderate heat. When the oil is hot, add the onions and garlic and fry stirring, for 5 to 7 minutes, or until the onions are soft and translucent.

Add the squid and fry, stirring occasionally, for 4 minutes. Stir in the wine, salt, pepper, oregano, fennel seeds and marjoram. Cover, reduce the heat to low and simmer for 1 hour, or until tender.

Meanwhile, make the tomato sauce. In a frying-pan, heat the remaining oil over moderate heat. When the oil is hot, add the tomatoes and basil and, stirring occasionally, cook for 20 minutes or until the tomatoes are pulpy.

Add the tomato pulp to the casserole, stir well, and bring the stew to the boil. Remove from the heat and serve.